OF SEASONS & SPARROWS

BISHOP KAY WARD

Interprovincial Board of Communication
Moravian Church in America

Of Seasons & Sparrows

Book design: Sandy Fay,
Laughing Horse Graphics, Quakertown, PA

Cover photo: Digital Stock. Used by permission.

ISBN: 1-878422-55-3

Printed in the United States of America

DEDICATION

For my family and my friends,

For saints and strangers and sparrows,

All who have seasoned my life,

I give thanks.

I am humbled by love, given and received.

To Diana and
Bruce –
How lovely to see
you – here are stories
for your journey!
Fondly
Kay Ward

FOREWORD

Thank you for allowing me the opportunity to share my journey with you through this book.

My journey is a small one. It started out as an angel in the Easter pageant. (The rest of that story is that my wings got stuck in the doorway of the house where we worshipped so I had to shout "Do Not Be Afraid" from the bathroom where I had been waiting for my cue.)

I came to love the Savior when I was a little girl. And very early in that love, I felt called to serve Christ. That service has changed and been shaped in many ways. As a lay woman, as the wife of a Moravian pastor — I'm still married to the most exciting man I've ever met, as a pastor of a congregation, as a teacher in the seminary and now as a bishop.

Many years ago, at a watchnight service I picked a text. (Or perhaps I should say that God picked a text for me.) I had come to that watch-night service feeling about as low as I had ever felt. I felt inadequate and unprepared for the challenge I was facing. I felt useless, and very unworthy. This was that text:

Not one sparrow falls to the ground without your Father's consent… So 'Do not be afraid,' you are worth much more than many sparrows.

I am astonished at the way God keeps finding uses for sparrows.

Kay Ward
October 2000

Table Of Contents

Winter

Spring

SUMMER

AUTUMN

WINTER

WINTER

A Generous Purple Sweater

Each of you must give as you have made up your mind, not reluctantly or under compulsion, for God loves a cheerful giver. 2 Corinthians 9:7

The month of January brings congregational meetings, new beginnings and thoughts of budgets and stewardship. Last Sunday, the pastor rightfully reached into the barrel of appropriate texts and came up with the familiar "God loves a cheerful giver," (2 Corinthians 9:7). It was a sermon with a new twist. Perhaps God is interested in not only how much we give, but in the way that we give. With what spirit do we make our pledges? Do we give with a generous and cheerful spirit? That was the sermon for Sunday.

Today I sit at my computer in my new purple sweater and I am thinking about that text — about God loving cheerful givers. Being cheerful givers may be the easy part. Being cheerful receivers may be more difficult. It is this beautiful purple sweater — a warm, soft, furry, luxurious, very extravagant sweater — that makes me think about being a cheerful receiver.

It was a Christmas present from our 19-year-old son. He arrived for the holidays with money in his pockets and a wonderful, generous spirit that directed us all to the mall on Christmas Eve for special purchases for each member of the family. Such an extravagant sweater is not something I would buy for myself.

I can't help but remember all those years of dragging our small children to dime stores and drug stores with dollars clutched in their hands to buy the other members of the family appropriate Christmas gifts. It was grueling work and we wondered at the time whether it was worth the effort to try to plant some deep seed of generosity in a materialistic world.

But now suddenly, those small children have become young adults and presents flow back and forth from one end of the country to the other as our family celebrates the holidays of gift giving.

I can't figure out where the time went. Just yesterday our son was giving me paper plates with the imprint of his hand precariously painted. Just yesterday our son was watching with anticipation as I unwrapped the toy soldier tree ornament made out of a clothespin. When did this happen? Where did this purple sweater come from?

There is, in the wearing of my beautiful sweater, a sweet sadness of years gone by when I got to do all the planning and most of the giving; when I got to be the one itching with excitement for Christmas morning when our kids unwrapped their surprises; when I got to be the one who could reap the harvest of a heart full of generosity and love. There was such blessing. God does love a cheerful and generous giver.

Now it is time to share the giving, the excitement, and the harvest. It now passes on to our children as they, too, can feel the absolute intoxication of giving a gift. Now it is time for me to practice being a cheerful and generous receiver. I've been practicing each time I've worn my beautiful purple sweater. It keeps me warm and makes me feel loved.

Thanks, son.

Giver of Life, make us generous and cheerful receivers of gifts, large and small. We thank you for the gift of your Son, Jesus Christ, in whom we pray. Amen.

WINTER

Kindness In The Fast Lane

Whoever speaks must do so as one speaking the very words of God; whoever serves must do so with the strength that God supplies, so that God may be glorified in all things through Jesus Christ. To him belong the glory and the power forever and ever. Amen. 1 Peter 4:11

It was a busy Saturday morning at the supermarket. Long lines snaked from each checkout. It was a typical day full of families with babies crying, toddlers having temper tantrums in the cereal aisles and unruly preteens embarrassed to have been dragged along for this boring outing. To make matters worse, snow was in the forecast. So every soul who had transportation to get out had come to town to stock up for the next "big one."

I joined the end of what looked like the best line to be in and of course that line immediately ground to a halt as market employees spread out in all directions to find the price of an obscure-looking package. My cart was full to overflowing, with large cartons dragging along the bottom and loaves of bread hanging precariously over the front of the cart.

A woman took her place behind me in line and we smiled painstakingly at the long wait ahead. Several minutes later, the groceries on the conveyer belt had still not begun to move and I began to calculate how long the wait would be. I turned to the woman behind me to make conversation, to fill the time. As I did, I glanced into her grocery cart. There nestled in the bottom of her cart were exactly 12 items, clearly exceeding the express line limit of 10 items and 10 items only. But this was a lady who would never test those limits.

Figuring 12 items couldn't possibly take more than a couple of minutes to calculate, I suggested she go ahead of me. I might not have been so generous if she had had 15 items and probably wouldn't have given it a thought if she had had a cart full of groceries, but there was something about the inequity of her 12 items that moved me.

She thanked me and we proceeded to change places in the line. We made small talk for a while. "Nice to have the sun shining for a change." "Yes, but did you hear we are supposed to have another storm moving in by the middle of the week?" And then after a few moments, she asked, "Are you a Christian?" I replied, "Yes, I am," but wondered to myself what difference that should possibly make.

My new friend was now nearing the checkout and here she really got energized. She tapped the lady in front of her on the shoulder as she was writing her check. "Do you know what this nice lady did for me? She let me go ahead of her. People just don't do things like that anymore." She now had the checkout person's attention and filled her in on the details and also told the man who was helping pack her groceries into two small bags. By the time I got to the checkout, everyone knew the story.

As I unloaded my groceries, I decided that this was a story with some bad news and some good news. The bad news is that maybe some of us live in communities where people just don't do that anymore. Such a small, trivial thing would be unusual enough to even be noticed. But there is good news too.

The good news is that, at least for this woman, there was an expectation that doing some small, good deed would be the kind of thing that Christians would do. She's right. We should expect people who claim to be religious to live out their faith in powerful and profound ways and also in small deeds that would go unnoticed in a better world.

Patient God, help us to be patient servants, looking for ways to comfort and love those we meet. May the light of Christ be made visible in our faces. Amen.

WINTER

Faith In Well-Loved Recipes

Therefore, since we are surrounded by so great a cloud of witnesses, let us also lay aside every weight and the sin that clings so closely, and let us run with perseverance the race that is set before us.
Hebrews 12:1

As a first line of defense against miserable weather, I enjoy spending time cooking and baking in the kitchen. I am especially drawn to those recipes that require long hours in the oven, so that both the good smell and the warmth fill the house. Last weekend we enjoyed Fran's Corn Casserole, Joanne's Whole Wheat Bread and Mary's Beef Stroganoff.

As I was cooking all these wonderful things, I was remembering the names attached to the recipes. These are folks who have given me one of their favorite recipes. For parsonage families who move so often there is a special delight in thinking of folks who remain part of the present, though decades have passed since we were last together.

But not only friends and acquaintances have supplied these precious recipes. Family members have offered their favorites as well. I can remember so clearly the little pile of white index cards that my mother carefully prepared for me before our wedding years ago. The cards are still in use in my recipe box: Ruby's Red Devils Food Cake, Grandma's Sugar Cookies, Mother's French Dressing. The cards are all spattered with bits of the ingredients, but mother's handwriting still guides my cooking bouts in the kitchen. These are the recipes from my family and my friends for a life of good food.

Now these significant people, the people whose names grace the recipe cards, who are such a part of our family, are being passed along to our young adult children as they begin households. Our daughter calls from California to quickly send Nancy's Fudge recipe and the pattern is repeated.

It is easy to pass these great recipe gifts on to our children as they have been passed on to us. I only wish I had been as diligent in cataloging the faith experiences that have influenced my own spiritual journey over the years. If only I had written down the faith stories of these significant people. Then I could pass them on to the next generation of our family. I would have a white index card that reads, Joy's Wonderful Outlook, David's Great Faith, and Bob's Power of Prayer. And when our son calls from California, having a bad day, I could send him Melody's Life of Hope. I could send him a card from my collection of recipes for a good life of faith.

And while I am at it, I wish I had written down all the beautiful hymns and verses of Scripture that have touched me and assured me of God's presence. I would have a white index card that reads: Paul's Words of Encouragement, Newton's Hymn of Grace, Sarah's Gift of Laughter and John's Words of the Cross.

And since I'm taking inventory, I should have jotted down what others have taught me about living with people. I would have index cards that read: Emma's Unconditional Love, Nancy's Code of Care and Brian's Getting Along.

But alas, I have kept no such recipes for a good life of faith, so I'll just have to improvise when someone asks me for a recipe. "You want Nancy's Fudge recipe? Well, along with the recipe, let me tell you about Nancy. She was in one of our first parishes and was one of the most joyous people. She loved music and when she played and directed, I knew that it was a ministry to God. I could see God in her music." "You want my Corn Casserole recipe? Well, let me tell you about Fran...."

Eminent God, we thank you for all the saints of our lives who show us your way and we thank you for your Son, Jesus, who is the way. Amen.

A Prayer For The Steelers

Rejoice in hope, be patient in suffering, persevere in prayer. Romans 12:12

The occasion was a gathering of clergy and laity in southern Wisconsin. The sub-zero temperatures hadn't stopped the 30 or so from coming to the church fellowship hall for a course on prayer, *When We Who Pray Become a Prayer*. Whatever had possessed me to suggest such a bold claim for a topic now eluded me. I looked out at the warm circle of faces and felt inadequate to the bone. The circle was made up of seasoned Christians; many of them had been mentors and teachers to me since my childhood. What made me think that I would have anything to say to these prayer warriors?

I opened the session with a comment about praying for the Green Bay Packers the previous week, the week they had lost the big game to the Dallas Cowboys. What had happened I asked? Were there more Dallas fans than Packer fans? Or were they just better pray-ers? Did quantity or quality matter? They jumped into the discussion with enthusiasm and we all had wonderful fun imagining the kinds of prayers that people do pray and whether God is really interested in football games. The discussion was playful. We all knew it was just a prelude to talking about the important things about prayer, like unanswered prayer, meditation and intercessory prayer.

A week later, the day of the Super Bowl, I was attending worship in a very large, rather traditional Protestant church. It was time for the pastoral prayer and the congregation was asked for prayer concerns. There were two or three immediate names of parishioners who needed help and healing and then a brief pause as the pastor waited for additional concerns. Suddenly, from the balcony came a loud voice from a new member of the church, a rather new Christian. “Let’s pray for them Steelers,” boomed the voice. The congregation responded with immediate laughter and then silence as they all looked to the pastor for reaction. “Maybe we should just pray for strength for both of the teams,” replied the pastor and he began the time of prayer.

There is a theological point somewhere in these two stories. The point may have to do with faith maturity. The old timers in the prayer course were saying much about their understanding of what prayer is or isn’t by playing with the idea of praying for football games. They understood that prayer was a matter of the growing relationship between themselves and God. Prayer came out of their lives and faith. They told stories of moments when they had experienced the rich miracle of knowing, feeling and hearing God in prayer.

The point also may have something to do with the new growing faith expressed in the church service. The young man’s new faith expressed the trust that when Jesus said to just ask for what we need, that included football victories. And maybe it does. It is refreshing to be a witness to that kind of trust. And while we always are being called to grow and change in our faith, to find new and deeper ways of expressing that faith, we have the opportunity to learn from and respect both those mature in their faith and babes in Christ.

We should have prayed for the Steelers!

Hearing God, we pray in trust for the needs of our lives and for the strength and wisdom to grow in our faith. Bring us closer to you, in your dear Son. Amen.

WINTER

GRATEFUL FOR THE FLU

Give thanks in all circumstances; for this is the will of God in Christ Jesus for you.
1 Thessalonians 5:18

I have the flu. And so does half the population, or so it would seem. So why should I be different? What would make me think that I should be exempt? With great effort, dragging my blanket and pillow, I move myself from the family room couch to the living room couch and in my feverish condition, I am bombarded with grand thoughts and questions about the nature of things.

For instance, I wonder if really important people get the flu. Does the Queen of England have an old pair of quilted slippers like mine that she wears to shuffle through the castle? Does her hair get all funny looking and does her head feel like it belongs to someone else? Does she ever hole up on an old saggy couch while the royal family stops by occasionally to view her, like some sea creature washed up on shore?

From a magazine cover on the coffee table in front of me smiles a sleek blond model. I wonder if she ever gets the flu? Does she ever suffer from a runny nose and bloodshot eyes? Does she drink gallons of liquids to wash down her myriad of medicines while her family spins around her frolicking and whooping it up with holiday cheer? It's hard to imagine.

I have the flu so it seems imperative that I watch daytime television, the kind of television that I never watch unless I am sick. It doesn't matter what the program is as long as there are little people moving in front of my eyes on the tiny screen. And I'm struck with how healthy most of the people on television are, except for a couple that seem to be terminally ill or recently murdered. But none of them has the flu.

I have the flu. And I wait patiently for the regular programming to be over so that I can see the next commercial. There, that's better! Over and over, every 15 minutes or so, I see folks just like me. Some of them look worse. They sneeze. They blow their noses. They cough. They look awful. They, too, have the flu and they offer me hope. Their puffy little faces earnestly sell their products, brand x, y and z, and I mentally check my medicinal stash by the kitchen sink to see if I've missed some possible miracle cure.

I have the flu and I begin to make a bargain with God. "If I live through this, I will never again take health for granted." Isn't it amazing that the days that we wake up in the morning without the flu, we often forget to thank God?

It is too easy to live our lives as though we deserved to be healthy and happy. We get so angry when something terrible happens. Terrible things do happen and it takes all the resources of faith to live through them. But having the flu is not one of them. Sure, it's aggravating and it upsets our plans, but it serves to remind us of just how good we feel the rest of the year.

We are encouraged to be "thankful in all circumstances" and I think the flu is one of those circumstances that puts us to the test. So when I am feeling well again, I certainly will be thankful and I'll try harder to be thankful each day that I wake feeling healthy.

But today I have the flu. Achoo!

Comforter God, help us to be thankful for the things in our lives and be merciful when we aren't able to be thankful. Give grace, O God. Amen.

WINTER

A Single Word Holds Many Meanings

Beloved, let us love one another, because love is from God; everyone who loves is born of God and knows God. 1 John 4:7

An article on Valentine's Day should be easy to write, so why am I sitting here staring at a blank sheet of paper? The problem is that the day calls for a piece about love. Love, that favorite four-letter word, feels soft in our mouth when we say it. At this time of year, we drench ourselves in the word. The word is everywhere. It glows in red-sequined signs. It dangles in windows. It marches along with the red and pink and white banners hurled in restaurants and shops. Love is definitely in the air at this time of year.

The word is so pervasive that we don't even have to use our favorite four-letter word. We can use a symbol instead. It's on our bumper stickers. I (heart) NYC. I (heart) cocker spaniels. Bright primary colored red hearts are also strewn liberally about the city in this Valentine week. Red hearts mean love so what is the problem?

Maybe it is a problem with our language. Native people in Alaska have many, many words for the concept snow. Some languages have many, many words for love. We are language poor. We have only one word. We have to resort to pictures and symbols and metaphors to help us say the word love.

We paint a picture of what love should look like — sparkling with diamonds, all bubbly with champagne. Love is portrayed by very thin persons with long hair entangled in each others arms. Our picture of love drips with roses and lace, and chocolate, — lots of chocolate. We sing songs of what love should be, songs full of lost love, broken hearts, puppy love, fickle love and love no deeper than a bird bath.

We have only one word for love and it has to serve all our different expressions of this very inexpressible force. At this time of year, it is very difficult to recognize love when we see it.

In the midst of long-stemmed roses, frilly cards and fanciful dreams of romance, there are those expressions of love that make all our glittered celebrations seem faded and superficial. This is the kind of love that doesn't make it into glossy cards. It is thorny, real and tough as nails. It is everywhere and unlike movie clichés, it can change lives. It does change lives, — every day, every hour.

Love is the quiet, utter contentment of a couple long-married, reading privately in the same room. Love is the steel thread that connects a parent and a child as that child moves out beyond the safe perimeter of the family. It is steel, yet it stretches forever. Love is the tedious, faithful caregiving for a partner who is dying. Love is the thorny confrontation that changes lives and gives second chances.

It is the transforming power that can make the weak strong, the poor rich, the ordinary brilliant. It happens all the time. Very seldom does anyone make a movie about this kind of love, or write a poem or compose a song, though some do. This kind of love gets stuck in your throat. It isn't soft in your mouth.

So maybe we are richer in language than we thought. Maybe there is power in having just one word, because each time we use it, no matter how trivial our attempt, there is the potential for life-changing love to occur.

I (heart) love.

God of love, bless all lovers and those loved.
Help our love be genuine and life changing
and let our love reflect your great love for us.
Amen.

WINTER

SEWING SISTERS

There is no longer Jew or Greek, there is no longer slave or free, there is no longer male and female; for all of you are one in Christ Jesus.
Galatians 3:28

The snow is blowing in horizontal blasts against the window. This old house does not give in to the wind easily, but moans and groans, in response to the raging blizzard. I sit in my favorite chair, a cup of tea at my side, all warm and content. In my hand lies a beautiful jacket, a sewing project for the evening. It is a jacket that I bought in Namibia in southern Africa, several weeks ago. It was made by a Namibian woman in a handsome African print fabric, but the sleeves are too long. My project for the night, while the snow bellows and blows, is to shorten the sleeves.

The first part of the project consists of removing the binding at the edge of the sleeve so I can replace it once the sleeve has been cut. I pierce into the tightly sewn seam and I am aware that the woman who made this jacket was scrupulously tidy and skillful in her work. I can see where she has carefully re-enforced the stitching so there would be no loose threads to unravel. My seam ripper takes each stitch out until I'm left with the raw edge but even here, my sewing sister has carefully made an extra row of stitching so the two layers of fabric will stay perfectly straight and together.

When it comes time to actually cut the sleeve, I feel a gentle tug at my heart and I am drawn into the piece of clothing. I am connected with that other place as surely as if I had been beamed up in some magical way. I can feel this other woman also cutting this same piece of fabric. She has made the first cut. I make the second. I can feel her presence, but I do not see her. This is an experience for feeling, an experience for the fingertips. That is where the knowing is.

My scissors separate a narrow strip of cloth from the jacket sleeve and, as the piece comes free, I am filled with the heat of a Namibian day. Her scissors must work quickly to finish before the shop closes for rest. The blazing sun is making its trek up into the top of the bright blue sky. The noonday heat makes her scissors sticky and the fabric clings to her arm as she leans on the table. Just the binding on the sleeves to finish and she will have another warm, quilted jacket on the way to the shop for tourists to buy. She smoothes the puffy seams and marvels that anyone would need a quilted jacket to wear. Where would such warmth be needed? Very far away she muses and wipes her sweaty brow. She wonders who will buy this one. Where will it go? There, the last seam is finished.

There, I have removed the binding on the first sleeve. I replace it in exactly the same spot only two inches higher on the sleeve. I leave her original stitches in the binding because they are so small and perfect. They must not be disturbed. And as I start to make tiny stitches of my own, I'm once again in snow-filled Pennsylvania and the Namibian heat is gone. But my sewing sister continues to be with me. As I try the jacket on once more to check to see if the length is right, I can feel her shoulders also trying on the jacket. We have both pulled it around us for comfort. We have both put our hands into the pockets. We have both smoothed the seams and straightened the collar. We are sewing sisters and the care and skill of this wonderful woman from the other side of the world, this sewing sister, will enrich my life for many years to come.

Holy God, we feel like very small creatures in a very large world. We thank you for the capacity to imagine and feel connected to your people wherever they are. We pray in the name of your Son and our Savior. Amen.

WINTER

As The Twig Is Bent

It would be better for you if a millstone were hung around your neck and you were thrown into the sea than for you to cause one of these little ones to stumble. Luke 17:2

Family night at the supermarket! I smiled as I entered, pushing my cart, remembering the times when our four children used to join my husband and me for a family outing, a fast food Friday night supper and then on to do the grocery shopping. This night I followed a family of four through the doors. Mom and dad with their two children, perhaps six and eight years old, the little girl still clutching her Happy Meal container. They were a strikingly attractive family with dark eyes and hair. The parents were impeccably dressed with expensive haircuts. The children wore comfortable stylish children's clothes and easy smiles. They exuded the confidence of healthy, happy, secure children.

I followed their cart up and down the aisles and what I heard in their conversation further demonstrated the genuine care that the young parents gave their children. Together they picked up ingredients for a Saturday baking project. Each took a turn deciding on their favorite meal for their one special assigned night of the week. Parents helped each child make good choices about healthy breakfast cereals and healthy snacks for school.

I thought to myself that this family was a good model of the happy healthy family. Though I couldn't be sure that things were always this way, it was apparent that there were some very positive characteristics of strong family values being demonstrated in this supermarket on a busy Friday night. With tired parents and tired children, the foursome spoke gently to each other and almost beamed with delight as they interacted.

We parted company at the dairy counter where I soon got distracted in the technicalities of four different colors of milk cartons and other challenges of modern-day grocery shopping. As I approached the checkout counter, I wondered if the family had already checked out. I didn't see them again until I had turned the corner with my cart full of groceries on my way to the car.

There they were, standing in a row, in descending order, first the father, then the mother, and then older brother and little sister. They were standing with their backs to me, but I could see immediately what they were doing.

In almost perfect choreography, they each reached out in front of them with their right hands. Father and mother reached out eagerly for the long strips of Pennsylvania State Lottery Scratchers, while their left hands fed in dollar bills. Brother and sister reached out eagerly for the toys and candy in the gumball machines, while their left hands fed in quarters. Their faces were strained. No one spoke until, just as I was passing, the little girl said, "Mommy, I ran out of quarters and I still didn't get the little doll with the beautiful orange dress."

The last thing I heard as I hurried to the parking lot was the mother saying, "Here are some more quarters. Maybe you will get lucky."

In addition to all the wonderful values being taught, these parents were also teaching their sweet children to gamble. I guess they weren't as lucky as I thought.

Father God, when we are tempted to stray from your will, help us to remember that small children are watching us be grown-ups. Help us to be worthy adults. Amen.

Making A Fuss

Honor your father and your mother, so that your days may be long in the land that the LORD your God is giving you. Exodus 20:12

Last month was my mother's birthday — her 80th — and I, being the older daughter, was prepared to do what I have done for the last 40 years or so; send a gift, a special book and a birthday card with roses or spring flowers on the front as well as call and wish happy birthday when the day actually came. But last fall, my sister began to pick up clues that something more was required for this birthday. My mother began to drop hints that this had to be a special birthday, so preparations for the event began. I made invitations and sent them out. My sister began to plan for the baking spree. Flowers were ordered and an appointment made to have our pictures taken.

Last month, after much rescheduling with career and family responsibilities, my sister and I found ourselves driving 18 hours through a snowstorm to be in Wisconsin for the party. And what a party — an open house at the church, with a decorated cake, flowers, pastel mints, punch, five delicious homemade desserts and flash bulbs marking each time a candid shot was taken. My mother, the birthday queen, worked the room, introducing us to all her friends as they in turn told us how lucky we were to have such a mom. We responded, "Yes, we know that."

The next day, we three women, making ourselves as stunning as possible, drove downtown to have our pictures taken. We giggled as we tried to relax, smile and hold still all at the same time. It was a good feeling to spend the 45 minutes in such close proximity to each other. Hands, arms and smiles were all tightly arranged for just the right effect.

It occurs to me, as I reflect on such a weekend, that my mother is even smarter than I thought she was, because she was right. We really did need to celebrate her 80th birthday in some special way. She knew something about what it means to be a human being and what it means to be a family.

Our family, like all families, isn't perfect. We are spread all over the country. We forget significant dates and we often unwittingly hurt each other, so it is even more important that we know how to celebrate once in a while. Not that such a little thing as a party on a Sunday afternoon would ever undo the hurts or make up for all the imperfections. Rather, setting aside time to acknowledge our love for one another can give us a taste of how things can be, how they will be, in the Kingdom and how we can experience shalom.

It wasn't a weekend for settling old conflicts. It was a weekend for telling stories as our mother and our aunt interacted with each other as they have for almost 80 years. My sister and I looked into the mirror of these older women to see ourselves and were pleased by what we saw.

The family gets knocked about these days. We forget to tell each other the stories about those times when we experience the blessings that a family can be. We forget to celebrate. We get too busy to throw a party. And perhaps we miss the kind of joy and sense of well-being that God really intended for us to experience.

Once again… happy birthday, mom… and thanks.

Peaceful God, shower us with the blessing of your peace as we celebrate our families. May our love for each other be a reflection of your love for us. Amen.

...And He Huffed And He Puffed

I am convinced that neither death, nor life, nor angels, nor rulers, nor things present, nor things to come, nor powers, nor height, nor depth, nor anything else in all creation, will be able to separate us from the love of God in Christ Jesus our Lord. Romans 8:38-39

It was Saturday morning, that moment of truth for preachers when all the little details of worship must come together. The biblical text had been chosen: Romans 8:38. The sermon had been written, with the point that it is only God on which we can depend. We can't depend on material things, people, or even powerful institutions to really make us feel safe.

It was sounding like a familiar story — the story of the three little pigs.

The first little pig built his house of straw — the stuff of our lives — and when the wolf came, he huffed and he puffed and he blew the house down. Just in case we are tempted to forget how fragile our material possessions are, every once in a while something happens; our apartment gets robbed or our house burns. One minute we have a lot of stuff and the next minute it is gone. Our house of straw comes tumbling down.

The second little pig built his house of sticks — the people of our lives — and when the wolf came, he huffed and he puffed and he blew the house down. The people in our lives are so essential to our happiness and well-being, yet every once in a while someone runs away from us, or stops loving us or dies. Our house of stick people comes tumbling down.

The third little pig built his house of bricks — the powers and principalities of our lives. And since life doesn't always turn out like a children's story, when the wolf came, he huffed and he puffed and he blew this house down too.

I love visual aids, so in my sermon basket — along with the clump of straw and the handful of sticks — I needed a brick. I called my neighbor and asked if she had one. She said yes; she'd look for it and bring it over. Fifteen minutes later, she appeared at my front door, carrying her brick in front of her in her two hands, like a warm loaf of bread. I knew immediately that this was no ordinary brick and asked her to tell me the story.

"When I was a small child, I couldn't wait to be old enough to go to the school, which was a block from our family home. My parents had attended the school as well as all my older brothers and sisters, and soon it was my turn.

"The happy school years passed quickly and soon it was time to graduate, leave our small town, marry and start a family. One day my father called to say that they were tearing down the school, but he had managed to rescue some of the bricks, one for each of his children. This is my brick."

I took the earthen treasure carefully and thought about the rest of my sermon. Schools are torn down, as well as churches and synagogues. My friend's brick stood for all those institutions that we are tempted to trust so completely. Even our houses of bricks sometimes come tumbling down. It is in God where we must place our trust and our confidence.

Powerful God, we are fragile people who look yearningly at our material possessions to make us feel safe and secure. Show us your strength and help us to lean on you. Amen.

WINTER

Respect Each Passing Age

For everything there is a season, and a time for every matter under heaven: A time to be born, and a time to die; a time to plant, and a time to pluck up what is planted. Ecclesiastes 3:1-2

The little girl in a pink baseball cap peered at me from the bottom right-hand corner of the cover of *Time* magazine. Her new, shiny adult front teeth looked too large for her little-girl mouth. A wisp of blond hair crossed her cheekbone. She could have been on her way to play a game of tag or to ride her bike to the schoolyard. She could have been off to play but she wasn't. She was on her way to an airport to pilot an airplane across the country. Her pink baseball cap said *Women Fly*, but this seven-year-old would never fly again. Her plane crashed. She and her traveling companion were killed.

Last week I had a birthday and along with the wonderful greetings from friends and family were some curious comments. "How many candles on your cake or is that a secret?"

"Well, no. It isn't a secret."

"Are you 39 again?"

"Well, no. Actually I am 54." I am not sure why my age should need to be a secret. I'm delighted to be 54. I have lived each year as well as I could and I can't imagine any advantage to deleting even one year from my history.

Both of these events, for Jessica to die at 7 and for me to be alive at 54, lead me to wonder how our culture views age. I wonder what age is really the age we all should be?

It's obvious that being a kid isn't the right age because so much effort goes into getting children grown up as soon as possible. Just being a kid doesn't carry the romantic, nostalgic glow it used to in an earlier generation. Terrible things happen to kids. They are decorated, coerced and programmed so they will look and act as little like children as possible. It is difficult to find that natural, carefree child of Norman Rockwell fame.

It is also obvious that being old isn't the right age either. Other cultures may actually revere and honor age, but despite AARP and other organizations intended to support senior citizens, our culture finds little value in old people. Like young children, old people do not have much power in a country that values power.

Being a teen certainly isn't the ideal age either. Rebellion, learning adult skills and that awkward search for self-identity make the teen years painful at best. There is an irony that our country's fast food places hire senior citizens and teens to work side by side.

Anyone who is over 55 and has tried to change jobs has found that all of the years of work experience make one almost totally unemployable. In fact the black balloons and dark humor of "over the hill" birthday greetings agree that it is at 40 that things begin to decline.

As you can see, this leaves only one golden decade that America apparently values above all others, the 30-somethings. Sitcoms are full of these talkative, playful folks who analyze their lives with a self-indulgence that mystifies their baby-boomer-plus parents.

Wouldn't it be lovely if kids could be kids and old people could be old and still be valued, respected and encouraged to attend to the gifts and graces of each stage of their lives?

Maybe 54-year-olds should wear pink caps and fly.

Lord God, help us to value our days in a timeless way, living in the present and being grateful for each stage of our lives. We pray through your Son. Amen.

Pastor's Wedding Gift

As God's chosen ones, holy and beloved, clothe yourselves with compassion, kindness, humility, meekness, and patience. ...Above all, clothe yourselves with love, which binds everything together in perfect harmony. Colossians 3:12, 14

It was a perfect day for a wedding, especially since the two previous days had seen the return of winter, complete with snow and ice and high winds. Now the sun appeared, melting the frozen, eager green shoots of early spring flowers. The ice and sun provided the perfect backdrop for this day of celebration. Weddings are occasions for celebration and reflection. The familiar lumps in the throats are made up of many things — regrets, joys, disappointments and broken dreams.

The father of the bride, stepping into his role as pastor, began by sharing the joy of this special day and expressing his thankfulness to God for the family who had continued to show their support and love, for friends who had enlarged that circle of love, and for a beautiful daughter who had chosen so well.

Then it was time for the serious matters of marriage to be discussed, the time when some wedding goers begin to squirm in their seats. It is hard to hear about the hopes and dreams of this day when marriages all around us fail, and when perhaps, even some of those sitting in the pews hold secret sadness. All the marriages represented listened to the words from Colossians. "Clothe yourselves with compassion, kindness, humility, meekness and patience... Above all, clothe yourselves with love, which binds everything together in perfect harmony."

We were being called to put on the wedding garments of compassion, kindness, humility, meekness, patience, and love, along with the bride and groom. We had all heard the beautiful words before and our faces flushed with the inadequacy of our relationships in the wearing of these wedding clothes.

The pastor continued by suggesting that he knew how difficult it was to live these words, and that he had prepared a wall hanging for the newly married couple as a reminder of the powerful words. He expected that they would probably keep it in the closet, but perhaps when they knew he was coming, they would take it out and dust it off and be reminded once again of this special wedding day. He explained that this was a wall hanging that contained the symbol of power for the American family. It represented the difficult matter of who holds the power in a relationship. It represented the hope for mutuality of that power that all marriages seek.

With great ceremony, he brought out the wall hanging from behind the pulpit. It was a rough slab of wood with the bark still visible at the edges, and at the very center was a black plastic television remote control. Everyone smiled or laughed quietly for they knew that the truth had been told. It is in the everyday living that our vows become tested. It is in the perfectly ordinary matters of who decides what to watch on TV or listen to on the radio, or where to go on vacation or what to name the children or where to retire, that the beautiful words get lived out. It is in the mutuality of those decisions that persons find wholeness and that marriages develop the strong fabric which can withstand the tearing and stretching of life. It was a fitting symbol for such a hopeful day.

God of our covenants, we are reminded of wedding feasts you prepare for us, as we come to our celebrations. Renew the vows we have made and make them holy. Amen.

WINTER

Moments Need To Be Counted

[Love] bears all things, believes all things, hopes all things, endures all things. 1 Corinthians 13:7

The building where I attend classes three times a week has five floors and a slow elevator. That elevator is a wonderful place to observe the drama of life being lived out. Since most of the offices in the building are medical offices, most of the occupants of the elevator have just come from or are going to a doctor's appointment of some kind.

I ride down with a woman perhaps in her late sixties. She is casually dressed as though she might go immediately to her garden upon returning home. There is an air of quiet about her as she descends to the ground floor. As the door opens, standing immediately in front of the elevator door is her husband. He brightens as the door opens and he sees her. He too, is quiet and careful and barely whispers, "What do they think it is?" "Nothing serious," she replies. His face visibly relaxes and almost produces a grin and he reaches for her arm to guide her to the waiting car parked in front of the door.

I have entered the elevator alone and the door is beginning to close as I hear running steps and an elderly gentleman rushes in just before the door closes completely. He is carrying a toddler flung over his shoulder. The little boy is sound asleep. They look alike, grandpa and grandson, but the boy has tousled blond hair and flushed cheeks. "They called to say they had an opening and he had just gone down for a nap," he said. I am struck by the care and safe keeping this little boy is receiving at the hands of a tender grandfather.

I am already in the elevator when a young couple enters on the fourth floor. He is clean cut, with chino pants and crisp cotton shirt. She wears jeans and a knit shirt which clings to her lean healthy body. There is so much intimate energy going on between the two of them that I feel like an intruder. They move to the back of the elevator and stand side by side, looking straight ahead, not touching or speaking. Words would be superfluous. As we approach the lobby, the young man reaches his hand over and places it on his wife's very flat abdomen. "Well, here we go," he says. She pats his hand and they float out the door.

The extraordinary thing about these acts is the lesson they bring: That in such a dangerous world, it becomes more and more important to count and remember such moments. They give us hope that love and care and tenderness does still matter and that we have the capacity to act with such courage.

Caring God, help us to count the tender moments in our lives. Help us to hold dear and precious the loving events that enrich our lives. Amen.

SPRING

SPRING

Wings To Fly

The creation itself will be set free from its bondage to decay and will obtain the freedom of the glory of the children of God. Romans 8:21

The religious community has long held out hope for the possibility of conversion as a way for human beings to change from what they have been to what they could become. Depending on our tradition, we use a variety of words to express that notion: rebirth, renewal, born again and transformation. We love to tell each other the stories of that religious activity, of how God was able to break through the usual barriers that humans erect. Our hearts are warmed by the notion of some cantankerous, snarly creature suddenly and inexplicably becoming kind and caring.

When that happens to other folks, the outward change is easy to explain. We point with awe at the brush with death, the power of a spiritual experience or the remission from cancer. The change in attitude and practice makes a lot of sense to us. We try to find stories and metaphors to help us talk about resurrection, and that religious activity — that change from physical to spiritual — which is so hard to express.

A transformation happened in my driveway a few weeks ago. This transformation in nature makes me wonder about the possibilities of transformation that humans might be capable of if we were more open to the spirit. Earlier this spring, we were given a cecropia moth cocoon and, frankly, we almost forgot about it as it hung lifeless on its piece of wood. Since it was a warm, sunny weekend, the cocoon was placed out in the sun and after several hours, the creature slipped silently from the cocoon. It certainly didn't look like a moth.

It was a rust-colored, furry, sticky lump. After another hour or so, the moth had begun to dry out a bit and the wings could now be recognized, though they were pleated and folded.

For the next several hours we watched as the moth came to life, very slowly at first, and then rhythmically, the wings began to move. It is such a human thing to use language like "come to life" when the cocoon itself was already teeming with life. What we mean is that we could now see the evidence of that life. The transformation of that caterpillar was a continuous process, but like so many things, we trust in that which we can see and experience with our senses.

Transformation in human beings is perhaps much the same. For many of us, spiritual growth and maturity is a long, continuous process and it may be difficult to see the potential in us at any given stage. Just as it was true with this beautiful moth, when the outward change takes place in us, we pronounce that the inner change has already been at work.

It took a whole afternoon for this beautiful moth to be ready to fly away. Many of us, who are furry, sticky lumps full of potential, stay stuck a very long time in our little cocoon on the earth. The afternoon in the driveway left me wondering. How did that brown worm know enough to soak up fresh air and warmth from the environment of our driveway so that the transformation could take place? How can our religious communities provide an environment of refreshment and warmth so that human transformation can take place? How did this sticky, brown worm know that it could fly? And why is it that sometimes human beings think they can't?

Transforming God, change us. Be the strong life force that can open us to new ways of being. Fill us with your spirit so that we find our wings and fly. Amen.

SPRING

LIVING THE WORD

All who exalt themselves will be humbled, but all who humble themselves will be exalted. Luke 18:14

Once there was a large, old church in the center of town. Its members felt called by God to reach out to their neighbors in some way. Each Sunday, the pews were filled with faithful members but most of them drove from their homes in the suburbs to the center-city church. They felt estranged from the college community that surrounded them. The boards met with the pastor and they wrote a mission statement to begin some new ministry. The first thing that they did was to make flyers inviting students to attend worship and tacked them all over campus. Nothing happened for several weeks. No students came.

But one Sunday morning, because it was bright and sunny, or because Bill happened to wake up before noon or had been having some unsettling notions about his life, he decided to go to church. He remembered the invitation tacked to the tree where he always parked his bike. He ran his hand through his long, unruly hair and dressed in his favorite attire: the T-shirt, with *This Bud's For You* on the front, his jeans with no knees and well-worn sandals. Bill ran most of the way so that by the time he reached the door of the church, he was out of breath and sweating hard.

Now, First Church was a church with a proud tradition. It prided itself on its marvelous music program, with Sunday evening organ recitals all through the summer. That proud tradition was also apparent in the way people participated in Sunday morning worship. Worship was dignified and in good order. Worshippers arrived well in advance of the service so that they could sit in their "reserved" seat and each was dressed in their Sunday best. Hats and gloves were still worn occasionally.

As Bill approached the door of the church, he heard singing, so he carefully pulled open the heavy door and felt a rush of cool air. His goal was to be as inconspicuous as possible so he started down the long center aisle, looking left and then right to find a seat into which he could slip, unnoticed. Not one aisle seat was empty. The last verse of the opening hymn was finished and all were invited to be seated. The congregation sat and Bill found himself standing in the center of the aisle, looking up at the high pulpit as the pastor began the morning announcements. Not knowing what else to do, Bill sat down on the floor.

The pastor greeted everyone and tried hard not to draw attention to the young man or cause him any embarrassment, but it was soon clear that the congregation was waiting for the pastor to do or say something. As he contemplated this, he noticed old Mr. Foley rise from his aisle seat near the back of the church. Slowly, he stepped into the aisle and began to walk the length of the church toward Bill. He leaned heavily on his cane with each step. Mr. Foley was an usher emeritus and pillar of the church, but his aging had caused some confusion and he could become very agitated when challenged by some new idea. The entire congregation was focused on this little drama, as Mr. Foley drew nearer and nearer to Bill. The pastor held his breath and decided not to intercept Mr. Foley, but to be ready to step in as soon as he reached the front. Bill wasn't aware of Mr. Foley's presence but could feel the silence of the congregation. As the old man reached Bill, he bent down, presumably to speak to the young student. But he didn't say a word. Leaning heavily on the front pew and his cane, he lowered his old bones and sat down beside Bill.

There was no need for a sermon that day.

God, help us to think of others, to put ourselves in their place and grant us mercy and humility as we try to do this. In the name of the One who came to be one of us we pray. Amen.

SPRING

FEEDING THE BIRDS

Look at the birds of the air; they neither sow nor reap nor gather into barns, and yet your heavenly Father feeds them. Are you not of more value than they? Matthew 6:26

My husband and I have become bird feeders. Well actually, we have become watchers of the birds who come to our feeders. After much advice from local folks, we've discovered the best place to buy bird feed. After many consultations with our friends who have a bit more experience with nature, we experimented with the best place to hang the feeders, and learned about the most enticing kinds of birdseed and what to do about the squirrels. In our case, that has meant finding a way to give the squirrels as much as they want and still manage to have some left over for the birds.

After all this preparation, we sat back to wait for the show to begin. "If you feed them, they will come," everyone assured us. They were right. It took about a week for the word to get out that there was a new deli open for bird business. At first just a few tentative sparrows appeared, followed by doves that cleaned up the fallen seed on the ground. In the passing of days, the following conversation began to take place.

"Any birds this morning?"

"Yup, there were lots of doves a minute ago."

Later.

"Lots of sparrows this morning."

"Sure wish we'd get some finches."

"Lots of finches this morning, just the purple ones."

"Wish we'd get some goldfinches."

"Anything interesting at the birdfeeders?"

"Nope, just the same old ones."

We had become bird snobs in a very short time. It reminded me of an occurrence when our children were little. Moving into a new house, we discovered that there was a window right by the dining room table, which would be perfect for a birdfeeder. Our three children were all in elementary school and we looked forward to being able to teach them to identify their new bird friends.

The bird feeder was put in place early one Saturday morning, and our youngest child, who was in kindergarten, couldn't wait for the first bird to come. He watched faithfully while the rest of the family went on to do better things on a Saturday morning. Later in the morning, we heard his delighted screams. "Come quick, a bird has come." By the time we all rushed to the window, the bird had flown away so Ben proceeded to describe his first sighting. "It was just beautiful. It had black shiny feathers and big round eyes, and a yellow beak and it was so big. Oh, I can't wait for you to see it." It wasn't long before the bird returned. It was big all right. In the Midwest, we called them starlings and we did everything we could do to get rid of them. I informed Ben that they were called starlings and he thought that was the most beautiful name, like something in the sky at night — starlings! I didn't have the heart to tell Ben that our first bird guest wouldn't be considered a welcome guest in most birdfeeders. He would learn that soon enough. For then, it was time to just put out more bird feed, lots of bird feed, which we did.

That story flashed through my mind as I thought about our conversation about the birds at our feeder. Perhaps it should be enough to have sparrows and doves or maybe even a starling or two. We'll try to be more welcoming to our ordinary feathered friends.

Faithful God, your eye is on the sparrow, and the goldfinch — and on each of us too. Give us the grace to see others as you see them, feathers and all. Amen.

The Queen Of Hospitality

Whoever welcomes you welcomes me, and whoever welcomes me welcomes the one who sent me.
Matthew 10:40

Business is brisk at the 24-hour convenience store. Small trucks wearing a variety of slogans back in and out while busy go-getters precariously balance large cups of coffee and hermetically sealed baked goods. There is a constant flow of cars filing through the two banks of gas pumps. Inside, serious young men in plain clothes stand beside young businessmen in three-piece suits preparing their cups of coffee to begin their workday. It is a place with a short attention span. Conversations are boiled down to one-liners. "Sure foggy out there, isn't it?" "Yep, but the sun will have it burned off in a hurry."

There are a few folks settled down over by the windows of the store where the booths are. They seem totally oblivious to the traffic flow around them. They are the regulars. They come in, pick up a paper and a cup of coffee and read intently, with their morning paper spread out on the Formica table. In the back corner, right next to the soda machine, a man and a woman sit facing each other in a booth. They each sit hunched forward, holding their respective coffee cups in front of their faces, almost prayer-like. Their eyes are just inches away from each other and even the casual observer is struck by the intimacy shared. It seems incongruous in this setting.

The reigning queen of the morning, the cashier, is a non-stop, all-business woman of indeterminate age. She greets each person directly, ringing up the purchases, while handling the gas credit cards and occasionally reaching into the meat counter to snag a hoagie. She works efficiently. No motion is wasted. She is entirely present to each customer, responding with a litany of "How's your mom?" "Is that a new jacket?" or "No donuts today?"

Every Monday and Thursday morning I join the parade of folks in and out to buy a cup of coffee. I do not know the cashier's name, nor does she seem to know mine yet there have been little snippets of conversations over the months of my patronage. That is how I know about the couple in the corner. "They're married. They meet each morning to have a few minutes with each other between shifts. He is coming home and she is on her way. Isn't that the dearest thing?"

Not much passes by the queen's notice. Last week, I made my usual Monday stop and as I approached the counter, her eyes lit up. "I have something for you," she said. "I noticed that you had a hippopotamus on your key chain and found this at a craft show yesterday." Shyly, she handed me a little pin with an endearing hippo painted on it. I was touched by her attention and it occurred to me that I could learn a great deal from my convenience store and particularly from this lady who offers such rich hospitality. She knows her little community so well and pays attention to the little details of our lives that make us feel like we are known and cared about.

It's just a little thing, but it would make such a difference if each of us paid that much attention to each other as we gather as the church. Think of the changes if we could all be part of a religious community that made us feel that we were known and cared about.

Welcoming God, you give us circles of love, of family and friends and community that show hospitality, that open their arms to us. We are grateful. Amen.

FINISHING THE RACE

And they said to him, "Grant us to sit, one at your right hand and one at your left, in your glory."
Mark 10:37

He was standing at the curb as we drove into the parking lot, a small pre-teen, sandy-hair boy, somewhat indistinguishable from the pack of other small boys. But his T-shirt caught my eye. Emblazoned in red on a blue background were the words, *If you can't win, don't play!* It seemed a very sad commentary.

Before I go off on a tirade about slogans on articles of clothing and bumper stickers, I must confess that there were occasions as our children grew up when I wanted to throw a bag over them, rather than reveal the message on a new shirt. But it seemed to me then, as it does now, that young people who are trying to grow up and separate from families, often need a safe kind of rebelliousness to help with the separation. Considering the kinds of rebellious activity from which young people can choose, we always thought it was fairly benevolent to just wear outrageous clothing.

Perhaps the young man at the curb was doing that too. But I was struck with the poignancy of the message and kept thinking of it the next day. *If you can't win, don't play.* As I look back on my life, the winning events were not the most memorable. In fact, the most satisfying things were often the activities that required teamwork. In high school, being in the band was a very important part of my life. It was the "being in" that was the important part for me. It is the being in the choir, being on the team, being with my friends. Maybe that is why we are called human "beings."

I know it is important for humans to be good at something, so at least once in our life, we probably should wear such a shirt. We all need to win once. It helps us know who we are. Families and religious communities can be the nurturing places where children learn about that kind of winning. Whether it is making the best paper-maché model of Solomon's temple or being chosen to sing a Christmas solo, people do need recognition as they mature. It helps to clarify the self-identity crisis that is part of the growing-up process. But if we wear the shirt all the time, it becomes a way of life.

The shirt says something so sad. *If you can't win, don't play.* If we really believe that, there is no opportunity to take a chance, to try something too difficult, to run the race when you know you won't come in first. It is comforting to know that even the closest friends of Jesus sometimes had a hard time with winning and coming in first. "Let us be first, when you come in your glory, one on your right side and one on your left" plead the brothers, James and John. Jesus answers, "whoever wishes to become great among you, must be your servant" (Mark 10:35-45).

Servanthood is about being with, and being in, and being there. It is about trying the impossible, even when we know that we can't succeed. It is about responding to a vision that calls us beyond ourselves. It is about wearing another shirt that says, *If you can't win, play anyway.*

Triumphant God, we live in a world of winners and losers. Help us to understand the difference between running the race and needing to win. May we look to Christ as the goal to be won. Amen.

SPRING

Polishing Shoes

Hope does not disappoint us, because God's love has been poured into our hearts through the Holy Spirit that has been given to us. Romans 5:5

I hate Mother's Day. It's a hard day for many of us. We are reminded of our inadequacy as mothers. We are reminded that we are too far away from our own mothers. There are just too many tributes, too many flowers, cutesy knickknacks and cards that say things that aren't congruent with the other 51 weeks of the year.

It's a day when it is easy to get caught up with the hype of the holiday, making promises that we cannot keep, and mouthing phrases that tell lies. One is expected to say wonderful things about mother on Mother's Day, but I want to say some wonderful things about my mother today, a week after Mother's Day, when I am not so tempted to speak in superlatives.

This tribute must speak the truth and look life squarely in the eye, in the same way that my mom looks at life. The tribute begins as soon as I enter her empty apartment in a small Midwestern town. It has a closed-up feeling and smells unused, as it has been since February when my mom was taken to a hospital with a badly broken hip.

What I notice first upon entering the tidy, efficient space is a flowering plant in the middle of the kitchen table. Over the years, many folks have given me these plants in bloom and mine almost immediately droop over the edge of the pot and die. My mom has had this plant for a year or so, and here in this still kitchen, it explodes with bright coral blossoms, twenty of them, each one outdoing the other. The plant is tended by mom's dear neighbor and friend. There is, in this plant, an extravagant optimism that fits my mom.

We talk often on the phone. She, usually tucked in for the night in her bed by the window in a health-care facility, and me, sitting on a long, narrow bench by my radiator in the dining room. The phone calls are essential for us now, to make the important decisions that must be made, to say the important things that must be said. My stomach knots as I relay the conversation that I have had with her surgeon. I try to find a good way to ease into the news that she will not be able to go back to her apartment and that we should begin to make plans for the future. As I am trying to get started with this sad news, my mom says, "Well, I really have never been very attached to my furniture." There is something so startlingly graceful about this that we can move on to speak of ways to make the transition.

She reports to me the activities of her day: working on a jigsaw puzzle, playing bingo, watching golf and enjoying visits and calls from her faithful friends. She also reports to me that the food is good; her caregivers are kind and attentive; the novel is enjoyable and her room is bright and sunny. I believe all of these things are true as she reports them, but I also suspect that if they were not true she would find a way to say them anyway so that I could sleep nights, so far away in Pennsylvania. I have never seen this generosity of spirit expressed on a greeting card.

On my last visit, I was given a list of supplies to bring from the apartment, including white shoe polish. I was so relieved to be able to do something for her. The next day I arrived to see her sitting calmly in her wheel chair in her sunny room, looking out the window. There on the bed in front of her were her sparkling-white walking shoes set carefully on paper towels, still damp with shoe polish, shining in the sunlight. They wait to be walked in, wait to be used again by a slowly mending hip. It is a gesture of sheer hopefulness. I never have been able to find that on a greeting card either. Happy Mother's Day, Mom.

God of hope, you fill our lives with people who inspire us. Help us to live as your people, trusting that it is in Christ that we find our hope. Amen.

Words Of Wisdom For Grads

The fear of the LORD is the beginning of knowledge; fools despise wisdom and instruction.
Proverbs 1:7

This is the time of year for *Pomp and Circumstance.* All over this nation, the familiar melody will be rendered on out-of-tune upright pianos and full symphony orchestras. The larger the graduating class, the more times it will be repeated. This year that familiar melody will have special meaning for our family as we attend the high school graduation of our son on one coast and the college graduation of our daughter on the other.

This prompts me to wonder what it would be like if mothers spoke at graduation ceremonies. Parents spend decades forcing their children to wear seat belts, nourishing them from the four food groups, keeping dangerous household chemicals out of their reach and reminding them to wear sweaters. Maybe it's time for a mom to give the commencement address! I offer this as a gift to our wonderful children.

How to Have a Pretty Good Life in an Imperfect World

Believe that people are generally good…
sometimes expecting folks to behave decently
is the best incentive for them to do just that.

Do something good for someone every day…
especially for someone who isn't likely
to be able to repay you in some way.

Learn one new thing every day…
 every 24 hours presents you with millions of facts
 and ideas that you don't know about.

Pursue a career that will provide you a living…
 but remember that you will never again feel as rich
 as you did the day you walked home with your first baby-sitting
 or lawn-mowing money jingling in your pocket.

Look for meaning in small events…
 rather than waiting for something extraordinary to happen to you.

Laugh at yourself much more than you'd like to…
 and at others much less than you'd be tempted to.

Invest in relationships…
 because on a cold, dark, sad day you'll need some warm arms
 to hug you and bring you cocoa and toast.

Understand your life as a whole…
 and care for your spirit as well as you do your body,
 or your car or your most-prized possessions.

Look kindly on the mistakes of your parents…
 at least until you begin making mistakes of your own
 and become compassionate.

Trust that the same gracious God that sustains your parents is also available to you…
 the relationship with that Grace is up to you now.

Your life will be about as happy and fulfilling…
 as you decide it to be.

Congratulations, graduate!

God of beginnings, stir in us the kind of earnest enthusiasm that we see in our children. Give our lives meaning, in spite of the pull of the world to make us feel meaningless. Amen.

Patterns Of My Life

For everything there is a season, and a time for every matter under heaven: A time to seek, and a time to lose; a time to keep, and a time to throw away. Ecclesiastes 3:1, 6

I am sitting on an old chair in the attic. The rungs are broken and it has been relegated to the "someday" assortment of furniture and appliances. "Someday" we will fix that broken chair. It is a rainy Saturday and I am sorting through old pictures in large boxes, searching for pictures, trying to find memories to take to a church camp reunion. There are piles to go through before I sleep.

The piles are my life and I am curious about the way the pictures have arranged themselves. Our wedding pictures lie among school pictures of our children. College pranks are tucked into the scores of pictures of Disneyland. Why did we take so many pictures of Disneyland?

As I sort, a poem comes to mind as clearly as if it were printed on the face of one of the photos. I first heard the poem when I was a sophomore in high school. We had a student teacher in our English lit class and I sat spellbound by her recitation of Amy Lowell's *Patterns*, the story of a young woman who has just been notified that her lover has been killed in battle, "in a pattern called a war." The poem was the most passionate, most romantic collection of words I had ever heard. And the beautiful, young teacher-in-training read the words so earnestly that I felt faint. The last line, "Christ! What are patterns for?" has remained with me all these years. Part of the impact may have been that I had never heard anyone say the name of our Savior out loud in school, even in a poem.

That line comes to mind as I sort through the pictures of my life. I sort through them to find some pattern. I try to find some way to bring order to our lives. But maybe that is impossible. Maybe the poem is right. What are patterns for — if death can steal love away? What are patterns for — if birthday children become adults who are no longer reachable? What are patterns for — if pictures of Disneyland no longer hold the promise of childhood dreams? What are patterns for?

Perhaps patterns help us see some plan for our lives. In seemingly random acts, life has brought us to this very day. There has been some kind of cosmic order, some gentle theme, which has threaded the separate events of our lives. I think there is a need for humans to look back on their lives to find the patterns that have composed those lives.

That reflective process is why I have pictures of each of our children on their first day of school as well as each year of carving Halloween pumpkins. I have annual Christmas portraits in front of the Christmas tree and children gingerly riding their first two-wheelers. These are the touchstones of my life. These are the pictures I sort through in the large box in front of me, in my attic, and they remind me of who I am and to whom I belong.

I think that's what patterns are for.

God of the Cosmos, you have brought order to a world of chaos and you bring order and peace to our busy lives. Help us to see you in the daily turnings of our days. Amen.

SPIRITUAL GARMENTS

Therefore take up the whole armor of God, so that you may be able to withstand on that evil day, and having done everything, to stand firm. Stand therefore, and fasten the belt of truth around your waist, and put on the breastplate of righteousness. As shoes for your feet put on whatever will make you ready to proclaim the gospel of peace.
Ephesians 6:13-15

Ephesians 6:13-15 portrays the spiritual garments that are resources for the Christian life. I'd like to suggest some additional garments, some wedding garments, for those of us who are married and who struggle to live in relationships as husbands and wives.

We will need some good sensible shoes that will carry us swiftly and surely from place to place so the two of us can be together. And we will need to take turns setting the pace — sometimes one taking the lead and sometimes the other. They must be sensible shoes, but we won't always wear shoes. Sometimes, we will be called to step into such holy ground between the two of us that we will need to take off our shoes. We will step into grief, into birth, into joy and into pain, and the space will be so intimate and we will both be so vulnerable that we will have to take off our shoes.

We will need a prayer shawl so, as prayer partners, we can bring to God the private things that the two of us hold in our hearts. As a praying spouse, there will be times when all we can do for each other is pray and that will be all that needs to be done.

We will need a full-length coat to protect our marriage and to draw each other under its protection. Marriage partners need protecting because we live in a world that isn't always good for us, that doesn't always value our commitment to each other. We are tempted from every side, and we are called as couples to confront each other, to step into conflict, to tell the truth and to protect our marriage.

We will also need a strong pair of glasses so we can see each other perfectly in focus. It is so easy to love people in general, sometimes even our spouses, but it is loving this particular person in this particular circumstance that is often hard to do. Our strong glasses will help us to do so.

We will also need a pair of gloves. Gloves will keep our hands warm and comforting for those times when we will hold and touch each other. Gloves will also remind us that sometimes we will be required to keep hands off — to be present but out of sight, to give the gift of space — to allow the dance to be led by our spouse.

As the last item of our wedding garments, I'd suggest a bright-purple hat — to wear for celebrations, to remind each other that there must be occasions to sing, dance, play and laugh with joy.

So here we are: all decked out in our wedding garments, but all the wedding garments in the world won't be enough. We can never supply all that we need, but we trust that God will supply the rest: wings on our shoes to keep us from weariness, the warmth of the prayer shawl, shades for our eyes to protect us from the harsh glare of the world, the power of our overcoat to comfort us, the wisdom to know when and how to be present, and of course, a feather for our purple party hat — God's final touch of grace.

God, our Protector, keep us safe in our relationships. We feel vulnerable and shaky as we struggle to live with each other. Help us to find safe shelter in a dangerous world. Amen.

SPRING

Framing Scenes Of The Heart

Again, the kingdom of heaven is like a merchant in search of fine pearls; upon finding one pearl of great value, he went and sold all that he had and bought it. Matthew 13:45-46

The painting arrived a little late for Father's Day, with a breathless note from our daughter in California. She hadn't painted anything for awhile and hoped we liked it. I was out of town when it arrived, but the minute I returned, my husband said, "Wait till you see what's upstairs." Carefully laid out on a table was a very large watercolor of a winter scene with a farmhouse and a wonderful wooden wagon filled with greens. It was lovely and it made us both smile to know that our daughter was happily painting again and that she knew so well what would delight us.

Getting things framed is something that we tend to put off, so we decided to be very intentional about this special gift, going down to the local frame shop the next morning. Choosing the right frame was difficult and before we were done we had a huge pile of mats and frame samples spread out on the counter. We enjoyed the conversation with the salesperson who was complimentary about our beautiful painting and we were struck with the beauty of a mural that encircled the small shop. It had been painted in the late 1800s and depicted the early community of the 1700s. We lingered through a wonderful gallery of art in the front of the store, and left feeling satisfied with our choice and grateful for the gift of living in a small historic town with quaint shops and friendly people.

Four days later, my husband called to tell me that the frame shop was on fire. It took me a minute to appreciate the significance of his statement. He went on to say that the owner of the shop had been working on our picture when she had to leave. The fire had started on the third floor and the fire department had contained the fire at the second floor but the entire building was full of smoke and water. The fate of our picture was undetermined.

The next three days were days of uncertainty. I reminded myself over and over that it was just a picture and that Melissa could paint us another one and that this was not a crisis that was eternal. As much as I reminded myself to not put so much importance in something material, I also had to claim the reality that concrete things can mean something beyond materialism. Certain concrete things connect us with matters of the heart. Certain concrete things connect us with spiritual realities, which is why, when we come to the Lord's Table for Communion, we use ordinary concrete physical elements. We are human beings who have the capacity for great spiritual depth and experience, but we often use the physical to hold those experiences.

This was more than a painting that we would put on our wall. It was a connection with our daughter, an emotional connection crossing the miles from one coast to the other.

On Sunday, we heard the news. Our painting would be ready for us in a few days. The volunteers from our local fire department had covered the paintings in the shop with huge tarps and were able to save them from the destruction of smoke and water.

The painting is proudly hanging on our living room wall.

Eternal God, help us to discern the things of our life that make us whole. Let us not be satisfied with cheap imitations of matters of the heart that are made authentic by your love. Amen.

SPRING

Being Waited For

So he set off and went to his father. But while he was still far off, his father saw him and was filled with compassion; he ran and put his arms around him and kissed him. Luke 15:20

This can be a time of year for sitting in airports waiting for family and friends to arrive. Recently I experienced a short three-act drama about being waited for. The first act featured an older couple, standing as close to the gate as they could. The man was dressed in casual golfing clothes with a camera on a strap around his neck. His cheery wife held a balloon that said *Welcome Home.* It bobbed frantically as she kept running to the window to watch for the plane. They worked as a team, checking the camera, turning the balloon around and returning to point to the door.

A middle-aged man in a dark suit played act two. He, too, stood at the entrance to the gate though a distance from the balloon couple. He seemed slightly anxious that the couple from act one would turn around and begin to talk with him, so he concentrated on a magazine. Occasionally, he would look up to see if the plane had landed, but all was done with a precision of movement. He was on duty and no one could accuse him of relaxing on his watch.

Act three took place around the corner where a young man stood. At first, it wasn't apparent that he was waiting for anyone on this flight. Then he, too, moved into place in front of the gate behind the businessman at a safe distance. This young man was unremarkable except for one thing. As he stood there, the corners of his mouth would slowly turn up and he would break into a huge grin. Then he would realize what had happened and would force his face to look serious again, but it never stayed that way. Clearly this was a man in love. The small bunch of flowers held tightly in his hand was further evidence.

The three acts all went on simultaneously, waiting for their cue to leap into action upon the airplane's arrival at the gate. The couple in front broke out of the line and raced to the window as the plane was landing. With his wife giving instructions, the husband took pictures with the camera still attached to the strap around his neck. The businessman, sensing that something was happening, folded up his reading material and reached inside his suit jacket for a piece of paper which he arranged carefully in front of his chest. It read *STALEY* in large bold print. The smiling young man gulped down the rest of the soda that he had been holding and fluffed up the flowers in his bouquet.

The doors opened and the first person through was a young mother holding a tiny newborn baby. With a diaper bag over one shoulder and the baby over her other, she struggled through the door as her elderly parents swooped down upon her, remembering at the last minute to take a picture of this transcendent moment, the meeting of their first grandchild. Some time later, a tall, slender woman, in a dark suit carrying an attaché case stepped through the door, scanned the area and finally fixed on the businessman. *STALEY* had arrived. They nodded to one another and the man held out his hand, palm up, indicating the way to exit. They didn't speak.

More people entered the terminal and by now the young man had moved closer and was jumping up to see over the crowd. Finally, there she was. Grin was met with equal grin as they embraced in place until the crowd moved them along toward the exit.

Three young women. All were waited for. But only two knew the human extravagance of having someone waiting for them with fierce love. I think that is how the prodigal son felt when he was welcomed home. This is the way God always waits for us. Welcome home.

Receiving God, we travel through our life always looking for a welcome home. In those moments when we turn from you, bring us back. Into your open arms, receive us all. Amen.

SPRING

A Cheer For Unsung Blessings

But he answered his father, "Listen! For all these years I have been working like a slave for you, and I have never disobeyed your command; yet you have never given me even a young goat so that I might celebrate with my friends." Luke 15:29

"He just went to work every day." I heard a journalist use that phrase to describe Cal Ripken's breaking of Lou Gehrig's record of 2131 consecutive games played. I am not a sports fan and can hardly believe that I am writing about such a record, but I was drawn to the historic baseball game and I, like so many others, watched the fans stand and cheer this rather shy, ordinary-looking hero for almost 30 minutes. The crowds cheered and whistled and slapped each other on the back. They held up signs. They kept calling Cal back out of the dugout for one more round of ovations. Reluctantly, he ran a victory lap around the stadium, touching many of the hands that reached out to him, especially the children who were there.

What a triumph! How badly we need heroes these days and how odd that this hero should be given a 30 minute standing ovation for going to work every day. There is certainly more to this story. Going to work every day for Cal Ripken depended on his being in top physical condition and on taking care of his emotional and psychological needs so that he did not get distracted from his job — a job he loved — playing baseball.

Such a celebration is a good model for us because we don't usually stop to celebrate the faithful perseverance of doing a job. One of my students told of recognizing a woman in her church that had taught the pre-nursery class of their church for 50 years. Once in a while we read stories of companies that reward employees for years of employment but usually such heroes go unsung.

The elder brother, in the much-loved story of the forgiving father and the prodigal son was one of those unsung heroes. And he challenged his father with his words. Many of us feel the same way. We often don't get rewarded for our faithfulness. And these days, when it seems that very little lasts, we probably should pay more attention to such records.

Marriages don't last very long these days so maybe we should take one worship service every year to celebrate the relationships that last. We need to be careful not to exclude those in our communities who aren't married or who live in non-traditional families, and we know that just because two people remain married does not mean that there is a strong, intact relationship, but we may have overlooked the sum of the blessings in our congregations. There are families who stay together. There are couples who stay married.

Maybe we need to celebrate those folks and let them do a victory lap around our sanctuaries while we all cheer and hold up signs. Maybe our cheering can help to support and encourage couples who are finding it hard to stay married. Maybe the church can be a spiritual resource for relationships and covenants can be renewed and blessed. Maybe some couples can set new records of faithfulness.

Cal did it. With God's help maybe we can too.

Encouraging God, sometimes we feel so unappreciated for doing ordinary things faithfully. Help us to live in our covenants and persevere in our ministries. Amen.

THE COUCH

You are the salt of the earth; but if salt has lost its taste, how can its saltiness be restored? It is no longer good for anything, but is thrown out and trampled under foot. Matthew 5:13

Twenty years ago, when our children were small, we bought a couch. It seemed an extravagant thing, but we all fell in love with it at first sight. As we were riding up the escalator at a department store it came into view. It was a loveseat, actually — beige with pale smudges of pastel colors — and we disregarded the practical warnings to ourselves that with four children a beige loveseat would not be a good choice. We bought it and brought it home.

Thus began the saga of our couch. We never called it a loveseat. For many years, it enjoyed a prominent place in our living room and earned the respect of our family for being the most comfortable seat in the house. Our little children snuggled there for stories, and guests quite naturally gravitated there. It had a cozy, warm appeal. Over the years, it moved from the living room to our family room where it became the favorite place for watching television or reading. No eating had been allowed at first, but now the rules relaxed a bit and smudges of pizza took their place among the smudges of pastel colors. It became even more comfortable and lived in as the cushions were pushed and shaped under sleeping bodies. Years later, it moved from our family room to the college dorm room of our daughter, then to our son's room, to a daughter's apartment, and then finally back to our house. After our last move, it got dumped in the garage. There it sat, with a spring curling from beneath the worn cushions, here and there a pale smudge of pastel color still visible.

Realizing that our children had great attachment to this couch, we announced our plans to find the couch a good home. Perhaps some one could find some use for it. There was a loud outcry from our daughter in California who looked into having it moved out to her along with several boxes. The estimate from the movers was over a thousand dollars. A shipping company said that it would only cost $700 to ship it, but we would have to build a wooden crate for it.

California daughter decided that she could get along without the couch. So we made plans to give it to a thrift store in town. We called several and several came to look. They informed us that the couch was too worn for them to warrant a pick-up. They suggested several places that might consider it if we drove the couch there to let them see it. By this time, we were beginning to lose our attachment to the couch. We were getting very anxious to get it out of the garage so that we could get our car in. We decided that we would just junk the couch.

We called the trash pick-up persons and they gave us the times, dates, categories and the costs they would charge us to pick up the couch. We called our regular trash pick-up folks who come weekly and they told us we would have to pay extra for any bags beyond our original agreement, but the couch had to be bagged. By this time we were getting desperate. We asked if we could somehow chop up the couch into pieces and put each piece in a bag one at a time. We were informed that if we did that, the chopped up pieces would constitute building materials and they couldn't be put in with our regular trash but they would give us the times, dates, categories and costs of picking up that kind of material. We gave up. And on a sunny morning this spring, we opened the garage door, dragged the couch out into the alley and left it there.

When we came home, it was gone.

Heavenly God, we are so aware that we are earthly creatures who have to live in our physical nature. Help us to give as much attention to our spiritual nature as we do to our material possessions. Amen.

SUMMER

SUMMER

A Small World

But Ruth said, "Do not press me to leave you or to turn back from following you! Where you go, I will go; where you lodge, I will lodge; your people shall be my people, and your God my God." Ruth 1:16

I am suspicious of clichés, especially when they seem to be true. They're just too predictable and give the impression that life is simple, orderly and dependable. When we say "It's a small world," we refer to the connection that we make with each other, the way that we relate to strangers and when we say it, we hope it's true. We hope that there is some kind of bond, some thread that unites us with people we've never met. It's a lot to ask of a cliché.

My flight had been canceled and I was stuck at O'Hare Airport in Chicago. It's fun to be in Chicago because there is a centeredness about the city. It draws people from both coasts and I was there, in the middle, standing in a long line, hoping to be rerouted on a later flight. Here are three of my conversations while I stood in line.

A stylishly dressed woman said she had to get to Frankfurt that evening or she would miss her flight to Kiev, where her elderly parents were waiting to pick her up, but it wasn't safe for them to stay in Kiev if it got too late in the evening. She said all this in one long sentence.

I asked, "Do you live in Kiev?"

"No, I live in California."

"Oh, I used to live in California. Do you live in LA?"

"No, I live in a tiny town on the coast. You probably never heard of it."

"My daughter lives on the coast. She lives in Laguna Nigel."

"You're kidding. That's where I live. What street does she live on?" We narrowed the geography and found that she lived three blocks from our daughter.

Behind us stood a marvelous gentleman, in T-shirt and bib overalls. He began to worry out loud that he hadn't been able to make a long-distance phone call to tell his nephews that he would be late. The longer he waited, the more anxious he became. To pass the time, I asked him where he was from. He volunteered that he lived in Eugene, Oregon, and that he was on his way to Wisconsin for a fishing trip. He came every year and his nephews made all the arrangements. I asked him where he was going fishing. Again we narrowed the geography and determined that he was headed for a lake about 20 minutes from our cabin in central Wisconsin and we had both frequented the same cheese factory.

A man behind the fisherman heard us say Wisconsin and joined the conversation. He and his friend were returning from a navy reunion in Colorado Springs and they both lived in Philadelphia. He continued: "I was in Wisconsin once. I'll never forget it."

"Oh really? I was born in Madison, Wisconsin."

"Well, that's where I was, on a business trip. It was quite a day, 23 inches of snow in 24 hours!"

"I remember that day and I can tell you exactly when that was — March 17, 1965. It was the only day in the history of the University of Wisconsin that they ever closed the school. My husband was a student there then."

"That's the day. I'll never forget it. We stayed holed up in a hotel until we could get a flight back to the East Coast."

We all looked at each other, and yes, we said it. "It's a small world, isn't it?"

Dear God, we yearn for connection and we cheer when we find ways to relate to each other. Help us to see ourselves as part of the whole human family. In Christ, make us one. Amen.

SUMMER

CATHERINE THE CALM

But I have calmed and quieted my soul, like a weaned child with its mother; my soul is like the weaned child that is with me. Psalm 131:2

Stranger saints can be found anywhere. There were about 20 of us waiting to board an airplane in Greensboro, N.C., along with 80 passengers who had arrived from Orlando. These were travel-weary folks, dragging souvenirs and luggage with sleepy children wearing mouse ears. The gate attendant announced our flight, asking for the twenty of us who had checked in at Greensboro to form a line to board the airplane. When that happened, the 80 Orlando passengers began to demand that they be seated first because they had left belongings in their seats. (This no-frills airline does not assign seat numbers.) They began to push their way to the gate until the attendant shut the door and demanded that they move back to the waiting area. The 20 of us were ordered to board the plane.

As I entered the airplane, I met my stranger saint, a young flight attendant who welcomed me aboard flight #553. She was a tiny woman with shoulder-length blond hair. She had a big smile and an even bigger presence. I warned this young woman that there were a lot of disgruntled passengers behind me and explained briefly what had happened. I took a seat in the first row, a seat that didn't appear to show any signs of occupancy.

Aware that they were angry and miserable, Catherine greeted each passenger warmly and gave each one her undivided attention. She acknowledged their frustrations, at one point saying that yes, it would have gone more smoothly if they could have boarded first, but here they were now and she would be glad to help them relocate and find their things if necessary. It soon became obvious that the other flight attendant had not yet shown up. She had had car trouble, so in addition to getting everyone seated, she now had to announce that there would be a delay. She did this professionally, apologetically yet with a matter-of-factness that was winsome.

Soon, everyone was seated and this charming woman announced that she was going to go out to the gate and get customer service cards for anyone who might want one. By the time she returned with the cards and distributed them down the aisle, most of the dissatisfaction had dissipated and few folks reached for the cards.

The tardy attendant finally arrived to the applause of the entire airplane. She received encouragement and attention from Catherine who urged her to go in the back and take a few minutes to collect herself. Once the flight was underway, she kept up a conversation with those of us in the front seats and we found out that she would be celebrating her 23rd birthday the next day. That news trickled back through the airplane and as we approached Trenton, the entire airplane broke into a rendition of "Happy Birthday."

Certainly many folks perform their daily assignments as efficiently and professionally as Catherine did on flight #553, but Catherine was doing more than just perform her job. She genuinely attended to each person under her care, and in spite of the angry circumstances, conveyed a confidence and joy that transformed the entire environment of that airplane.

Transforming God, help us to remember that we have the capacity to change our environment with a calm spirit, a tender word, a gentle touch. Make us instruments of your peace. Amen.

SUMMER

Making A Life

My child, do not forget my teaching, but let your heart keep my commandments; for length of days and years of life and abundant welfare they will give you. Proverbs 3:1-2

This is written as a public service for parents and children who are 50 percent through summer and 100 percent through all the good ideas that were going to fill the long days of vacation with meaningful activities. It may also be helpful to anyone who finds a little too much time on their hands or someone who hasn't taken the opportunity to spend a meaningful, playful hour or two for their own mental health. In an era of leisure time that gets booked as solidly as our work hours, it has been said that we play at our work and work at our play. When the ability to entertain oneself is not a valued skill and when not spending money or using technology to entertain is considered odd and rather suspect, I offer these methods for something to do when there is nothing to do. These activities may be done alone or with someone, do not cost more than $5.00 and in some small way, may contribute to making the world a better place to be. I call it "Making a Life."

1. Find your local library and get a library card.

2. Go to the nearest toy store, buy the cheapest kite you can buy and one ball of string and go fly it.

3. Read the Gospel of Mark.

4. Wash and polish your bike or your motorcycle or your car.

5. Borrow a five-year-old and take him or her to the park to play.

6. Write to your grandmother, aunt or cousin and tell them how important they are in your life.

7. Set yourself a goal of living one whole Saturday without TV and without spending any money.

8. Go to the library and pick someone out who is looking for books and looks interesting to you. Ask them to tell you the best book they have read in the past year and check it out and read it.

9. Call the Chamber of Commerce in your town and ask them to tell you about the tourist attractions that you shouldn't miss in your own town. (Go only to those with an admission cost under $5.00.)

10. Set the alarm and get up to see the sunrise and then spend time thanking the Lord who made it.

11. Buy two "slice-and-bake" rolls of cookies and take some to your neighbors.

12. Buy a small box of crayons and draw a picture.

13. Go to your local playground or park and watch a Little League or soccer game.

14. Buy a handful of postcards from your town and send them to people you know who are on vacation. Tell them what a wonderful summer you are having and send them a "wish you were here" message.

15. Think about an important person who you have heard about with the same first name as yours and go to the library and find out all about him or her.

16. Write a short essay on *what I did on my summer vacation* so that you are all ready to go back to school.

Recreating God, we fill our lives with so many things to do and yet we don't feel we have done anything life giving or renewing. Help us to use our precious, leisure time to refresh our minds and bodies. Amen.

SUMMER

Hearing God In The Quiet

"Be still, and know that I am God! Psalm 46:10

Sitting on the steps of my log cabin, I have given myself the morning to listen to the quiet of the woods, just to listen, observe and write down what it is that I have come to find on my vacation. I know I needed to get away and this is the morning I am considering what it is that I was getting away from.

The summer has been cool in Wisconsin and this morning the sweat-shirt feels good as I sit in a sunny spot on the step to enjoy my morning coffee. There is a slight breeze. My first impression is how quiet and still the woods are. The sun shines through the birches and maples to my left, making distinctive light and dark patterns on the woods below. At first I hear no noises, no voices, but as my ears become accustomed to the quiet, I discover that it is not an absence of sound that I hear. Rather it is a purposeful quiet and I begin to hear the woods' sounds of life.

A swallow swoops, a chipmunk scurries among the leaves and now that I have settled myself to listen, I hear not only the sounds of nature, but the muffled sounds of the world too: a small airplane buzzing overhead and the far-away sound of a truck on the highway.

The quiet of the woods is not an absence of sound. We are not in a vacuum. In fact, the woods are not still. But it is very different from the sounds of the rest of my life. Here the sounds demand nothing of me. No telephone rings demanding my response. Traffic doesn't distract with its message of having to be somewhere. There are no memos in my mailbox. In fact, there is no mailbox. The quiet I have come seeking is one of calm stillness, rather than the absence of sound at all. But it is not an absence of activity either, for the woods make its own demands of me.

The woods draw my attention. When I am thirsty, I must pump water. When I am cold, I must carry in wood and start a fire. When I hear a new bird sound, I am drawn to the location. Flowers, butterflies and even tiny tree toads draw me to them.

God calls us through the Old Testament text, "Be still and know that I am God." One doesn't need the woods or even a vacation to step into that kind of stillness. The human spirit has the capacity to be drawn into stillness anywhere, anytime, but it always seems easier here, away from the rest of my life. The woods teach me that being still is not so much a denial of the things that I do in the rest of my life, but rather an invitation to another level of living — the small, delicate dancing of leaves; the intentional crawling of ants; the lifting of a bird's wing in flight. This paying attention to the ordinary, to the natural, can call us to a still, small place where God comes rushing in, to soothe and refresh.

My coffee cup sits empty and I am called to the woodpile. It will be a cool evening. The woodstove needs attention.

Refreshing God, you call us in so many ways, but we often don't make a place in our lives to hear you. Help us to create sacred empty spaces where we can hear and obey your calm voice. Amen.

The Sound Of Sheer Silence

Now there was a great wind, so strong that it was splitting mountains and breaking rocks in pieces before the LORD, but the LORD was not in the wind; and after the wind an earthquake, but the LORD was not in the earthquake; and after the earthquake a fire, but the LORD was not in the fire; and after the fire a sound of sheer silence.
1 Kings 19:11b-12

It is sunset on a cool evening in the woods and I am sitting on the screened-in porch, deep into a book. It is a book saved for vacation, with many, many pages, each full of lush descriptions and lilting dialogue. It is *Beach Music* by Pat Conroy. The music of the woods played its part, accompanying the words on the page as they formed in my mind. The woods music remains a mystery to me. Who makes those little chirping deep-throated sounds or the warbles overhead? Visiting friends have identified those warbles as sandhill cranes, but there are multiples of other voices. Their voices echo back and forth from tree to tree. A small woodpecker explores a big old birch trunk, methodically hammering at intervals for a choice bug. His method is rhythmic and hollow as it reverberates on the old trunk.

There is movement too, that makes sound. Tiny chipmunks make more noise than they seem able, as they scurry up and down logs, scattering grasses and small twigs. Squirrels chase each other from one limb to another in some carefully choreographed chase. It is a 10-ring circus of climbing, leaping and flying.

A background for the woods music is the world music. It becomes louder as the evening breeze shifts and carries the sounds our way.

Huge trucks shift and groan as they make the right-hand turn onto the county road. Tractors putt their way down the farm lanes, done for the day and heading to a refreshing summer supper. Overhead, a small airplane circles as it prepares for descent into the tiny airport in town. Far away, yet still audible, is the drone of a crop duster blanketing the potato fields with insecticide. Voices of children playing come and go, like someone is turning the volume up and down on a radio. Even the log cabin creaks and snaps with the cooling of the evening. Whoever said that the woods was quiet was not on my porch on this particular night, but the woods music is soothing and pleasant.

Several chapters later, I suddenly raise my head and notice that at the very same moment my husband, who was reading next to me, also raises his head. Something dramatic is happening almost instantaneously. The woods music is stilled, absolutely stilled. Leaves, just moments before jostled by squirrels, are now motionless. It is a stillness that is so audible that it breaks into our concentration. It demands our attention.

The text for morning worship on our first day back from vacation was from 1 Kings 19:7-13, Elijah meeting God on Mount Horeb. Elijah, in the midst of his own woods music, hears God in a still, small voice. First a great wind, then an earthquake, then a fire. But the Lord wasn't in any of that music. "After the fire, [there was] a sound of sheer silence." (1 Kings 19:12b) The sound of sheer silence was so loud that it got Elijah's attention.

What I experienced on our porch is even more precious these days when it is often hard to hear God in our lives. It is tempting to want to stay in the silence. But even Elijah didn't get to enjoy the sound of sheer silence very long. God used the silence to woo Elijah. Once the Lord had his attention, Elijah was instructed to return to his calling. He had some king anointing that needed to be done. Back to work. Back to the world's music, which is where we all live, move and have our being.

Persistent God, you woo us in so many ways.
You call us with a shout or a whisper or
whatever we need to turn our attention to you.
Thank you for calling us. Amen.

STORAGE SHEDS

Do not store up for yourselves treasures on earth, where moth and rust consume and where thieves break in and steal; but store up for yourselves treasures in heaven, where neither moth nor rust consumes and where thieves do not break in and steal. For where your treasure is, there your heart will be also. Matthew 6: 19-21

Each summer our family returns to the small Wisconsin town where we lived in the early '70s. It has been interesting over the years, to watch the town grow as shopping malls have replaced the mom-and-pop shops of the past. Fast-food restaurants have replaced most of the diners and small eating places. The old movie theater now shows four films at a time and familiar roads and bridges have been replaced with bypasses and one-way streets. All in all, the town has grown well, welcoming new establishments that will more adequately meet the needs of the current residents.

For those of us who vacation there, it gets harder to find a laundromat or a place to buy kerosene, but all in all we, too, enjoy the progress that has been made. But this past month, we witnessed the newest of the changes in the town, an addition that moves the town into big American city status.

On the outskirts of town, out beyond the lake front homes with pine-tree-covered front lawns, past the first few farms, but before you come to the potato fields, a new building was being constructed. Our first week there, we noticed the foundation being poured, and soon after, the framing took place. We speculated what the structure might be. It was long and narrow and at first we guessed that it might be a new motel for the variety of tourists that find Wisconsin the perfect vacation spot. But soon the structure took shape and we could see what it would become — another of those wonderful storage units that have become an essential part of the American way of life. To be truthful, I dare not be too critical of something that I may personally find useful some day, but it did occur to me that the storage unit is a perfect metaphor for the kind of lifestyle that we enjoy.

I have sometimes been embarrassed when entertaining guests from other countries as they experience the amount of stuff our family has accumulated and the amount of space that we have to fill with that stuff. It is a luxury to have material possessions and the space to hold them. Certainly there are occasions when families in transition need a place to store furniture and household possessions, but I would guess that most units are filled with our kind of overflow. It is the kind of overflow that fills my own drawers and closets and a very large attic.

Perhaps what is troubling about building storage units in a small town in Wisconsin is that it encourages a bad habit. We are already so tempted to hoard and buy and have, that building a storage unit is a bit like serving alcohol to an alcoholic or sponsoring a lottery for folks who are addicted to gambling. We need all the help we can get to put first things first and not to be so consumed by our possessions. A storage unit was one thing that I think our small town in Wisconsin could have done without.

Sufficient God, we are privileged people and we find it hard to not want more than we need. Fill our hearts and spirits so that we won't be tempted to acquire more things. Amen.

SUMMER

Shapes Of The Father's House

That one is like a man building a house, who dug deeply and laid the foundation on rock; when a flood arose, the river burst against that house but could not shake it, because it had been well built.
Luke 6:48

There is a cabin in the woods, built with slabbed pine logs and rough-cut lumber. It looks exactly like the kind of houses that children draw, with its peaked roof and a tall stone chimney at one end. Square windows are symmetrically placed on each of the sides and there is a plank door at the front and the back with the same number of steps leading upward. It is built in the middle of a deep woods and looks as if it is trying to pull the woods over its head. It is authentic and practical and has a no-frills air about it that gives the impression that nothing could uproot it from its attachment to the earth.

There is a house on the bay, built with cedar and heavy wooden beams. It doesn't look like a house at all, with its soaring walls and angular living space. It is, in fact, a cube set into the ground on one point, rising like some wonderful sculpture with surprises for windows and lofts with footholds for adventurous guests. It looks like a giant building block with wings, hanging over the edge of a rocky cliff, with the spray of the lake on its face and the wind in its ears. It is futuristic and breathtaking and gives the impression that at any moment it might leave its earthly existence and become airborne.

The cabin in the woods is our vacation home and the house on the bay is our friends' vacation home. When we built our cabin 20 years ago, we read everything we could about log cabins. We looked at pictures and studied how they were constructed and tried to replicate every detail so that our cabin would look like a real log cabin. We were drawn to the inconspicuous homey look, and when it was finished, everyone agreed that it looked just like a real log cabin.

Our friends, on the other hand, pictured in their minds a beautiful soaring shape that would become their house. They even made a model of the cube shape so that we could picture what it would look like when it was constructed. Since no one had seen a house like this, they consulted designers, architects and builders to determine if such a house could be built. And then they went to work, using ingenuity to find ways to shingle the huge surfaces which were both roof and side walls of the structure. When it was finished, everyone agreed that it was the most unique house anyone had seen.

What is interesting about these two houses is that they were built by folks with much in common. Both families had the need for a place that would be a home for them in the years to come, but that need was met in very different ways. These kinds of differences aren't only discovered in building houses. In our communities of faith, we often experience conflict when we try to build our expression of what the church should be.

Those of us who are the traditionalists know what a church should be by looking at how it has always been. We want it to act like the church we have always known. We want things predictable and safe, with no conflict. Those of us who are visionaries know what a church should be by imagining ways it has never been and moving toward that vision. We want change and renewal and we are willing to live with the tension that results.

The truth is that we need both traditionalists and visionaries in order for the church to continue healthily. We need log cabins in the woods and houses on the bay.

Eternal God, help us to live with one another as the church. Let differences make us stronger and give us a taste of your kingdom here on earth. Amen.

SUMMER

Too Many Choices

Choose life so that you and your descendants may live, loving the LORD your God, obeying him, and holding fast to him. Deuteronomy 30:19b-20a

I think the best part of vacation is doing something different from the ordinary things you do the rest of the year. That's the idea, but it sometimes doesn't turn out that way. For many women, vacation means shopping, cooking and doing laundry — but doing these chores in a beautiful, though less convenient, place. So in thinking back over my vacation in Wisconsin, the most surprising thing came to mind as one of the most restful things that happened.

What I have remembered are the trips to the little grocery store in the village near our cabin. It is in a town of 350 people. Attached to the grocery store are a meat market, a tavern and a bowling alley. This is a no-frills grocery store with only four short aisles worth of groceries. After the first couple of visits to this dear store, I stopped making a menu for meals with food I wanted and started to make a menu with food they had. It was just so much easier. Like the grocery store in Garrison Keillor's *Lake Woebegone*, if they didn't have it, I didn't need it.

The merchandise is carefully chosen to supply good home-cooked meals. There is a soup section, Campbell soup, with the soup you need — tomato, bean with bacon, chicken noodle, vegetable and cream of mushroom — lots of cream of mushroom. No low-fat, low-sodium healthy soup, no consommé, and no cutesy little pasta-shaped soup, just the basics. It's the same with the peanut butter:

one brand — Skippy, creamy and crunchy. Soap, paper towel and catsup selections are no different. There are few choices to make in this store and it is surprisingly relaxing.

We live in a culture that affirms "choice" as the most valuable human right. A large supermarket has more than 25,000 items to choose from. There are over 11,000 magazines and periodicals, and cable television offers us more than 50 channels from which to choose. Even in the relative simplicity of my log cabin, I am beset with the endless choices of life: Morning coffee used to be a matter of boiling lots of dark coffee grounds from a can — not a bag — in a large percolator with the little glass bubble on top. Now we make decaf coffee, caffeinated coffee and two kinds of flavored coffee, in a drip-through filter or an infuser. That is why the experience of shopping in the little grocery store is such a refreshing change.

My husband and I experienced that same kind of refreshing change when we traveled in Africa. We took most of our meals on the road in little shops or restaurants and the choices were simple. Small blackboards on the wall announced sandwiches: cheese, cheese and ham, or cheese and tomato. You told them which one you wanted. They didn't ask what kind of bread, or whether you wanted mustard or mayo. They didn't offer the chance to have it your way and it was surprisingly simple and calming. In very nice restaurants, the entrees were listed precisely — chicken, beef, wild game or fish. They didn't ask for your choice of dressing on the salad or kind of potato. They made up a plate and gave it to you.

I realize that I am treading on dangerous ground here, because I don't want my right to make choices taken away, and I love all of the variety of new healthy products that line my grocery aisles. But I do experience a kind of simple abundance when I am met with a minimalist approach to shopping. Maybe we have too many choices. Maybe so many choices add to the stress of our lives. Maybe we do need only five kinds of soup.

God of simplicity, we are people of complexity. Help us to sort out the essentials of your life for us and give us discernment in all choices and decisions. Amen.

SUMMER

Rose-Lined Country Roads

Now there are varieties of gifts, but the same Spirit; and there are varieties of services, but the same Lord; and there are varieties of activities, but it is the same God who activates all of them in everyone. 1 Corinthians 12:4-6

With folks hitting the road for long-awaited summer trips, it occurs to me that there are two kinds of people, actually two kinds of drivers, in the world. There are those who pride themselves on getting in the car, finding the shortest distance, via the largest available highway, and arriving in the shortest possible time. These are the folks who keep personal "bests" for familiar distances and speak with pride when they cut off a minute or two from their previous records.

Then there are those who call it a successful journey if they have investigated every gravel lane and country road on the way to a particular destination. They pride themselves on finding a small two-lane asphalt road that runs parallel to the freeway or interstate so that they can see more things.

These two drivers have totally different goals. The first, "make straight a highway" kind of person measures speed and directness as the goal. Getting there quickly is the goal. The second measures by how much is seen along the way.

It is tempting to categorize people. It helps us put people in a place and gives us the impression that we might be able to predict what they will do. Understanding how people go about the ordinary tasks of their day is a complex activity, and we look for shortcuts to understanding. My sister-in-law says that you can tell a lot about people by just watching them read the Sunday paper. Do they head for the sports page, the comics or the front page? This could be very important information if you were picking a mate.

There are differences in the way we approach our daily routines, and the way we view the world. There are ways that we naturally go about things. While I want to think of myself as a creative, spontaneous, meandering kind of explorer, the truth is, I'm the "make straight a highway" kind of person when I drive. I want to think of myself as the kind of person who takes time to stop and smell the roses, but in truth, I don't usually even see the roses, to say nothing of stopping and smelling them.

Our differences have a lot to do with the way we live our spiritual lives, too. My spiritual journey is usually as frantic and fast as any of the other journeys I take. I want spiritual maturity to happen quickly. I want to get there. I don't want it to take time. It is as difficult for me to slow down, be quiet and wait on the Lord as it is for me to choose country roads to get where I am going. My hope is that through grace we are offered a variety of ways to come to God. The traditional spiritual disciplines work very well for many Christians, but I keep looking for those unexpected joys, those blinding insights, those larger-than-life experiences that will catch my eye as I speed along on my spiritual journey. And the blessing is that they are often there.

Safe travels, friends.

God, you are our Guide as we travel through life. Help those of us who travel so quickly to find ways to slow down. Help all of us to be open to the surprises that you offer. Amen.

SUMMER

Escape From Sameness

Those who wait for the LORD shall renew their strength, they shall mount up with wings like eagles, they shall run and not be weary, they shall walk and not faint. Isaiah 40:31

The view from my log cabin window is still etched in my mind as I start back to work. That view lingers, though the particularities of my vacation have begun to fade. This year, Wisconsin in August was a lush extravagance of green. Having enjoyed a very wet July, our woods were almost fluid with delicate ferns displaying the moisture. Our large old trees were alive with the adventure of being green. It was the greenness that greeted me as I framed the woods in my bedroom window — a green carpet of tall grasses, small, green bushes and shrubs filling up the space till they met the tall, green canopy of oaks, maples and pine. And there in the picture — in my window frame, about one-third of the way up at the top and to the right — was a brilliant branch on one of the younger maples surrounding the cabin. The colors ranged from red to gold to orange and in the midst of the green, it seemed to be aflame. It was, of course, the stunning contrast that made it seem so. That same branch in the midst of autumn color would not have been extraordinary, but here it was, out of sync with the rest of the woods and breath-taking to behold.

I pointed out my treasure to several of our friends as they visited and they offered theories as to why such a thing should occur. Some said that it was the dry June and the wet July that had tricked the tree into thinking it was fall. Most said it meant the tree had some dreaded disease. But, of course, they were not seeing it as I saw it out of my bedroom window.

What I understood as I looked at this bright and shining branch of color swimming in the green, was a wonderful way for me to understand what vacations, holidays and sabbaths are really about. The branch became an expression of the escape from sameness. The human heart hungers to escape from sameness. We go to great effort to plan our lives so that we can do something different when we have time off from our labor. We go off on canoes and paddle lazily. We go to museums and enjoy the hustle and bustle of a large city. We stay in places that are not at all like our other life — places like a log cabin, with water from a hand pump, light from dim kerosene lamps and plumbing (or the lack thereof) in the woods.

And wonder of wonders, we find ourselves relaxing and being refreshed, even though we may still find our hours filled from sunup to sundown. It is the escape from sameness that can renew. God's gift to us in creation is that we can be re-created again and again by these tiny little escapes. We may call them recreation, re-creation. And whether we are fortunate to have a week or so to escape, or whether we steal away for a day or two, or even if we just are able to find an hour or so, we still can plan something good for our spirit that grants us the tiny escape from sameness. And like that brilliant branch of color, we find our spirits rising. Our senses are revived and we can begin to feel good again.

Renewing God, we are made weary by our
tedious lives and we long for some new thing.
Make us a new creation each and every day.
We praise you for making all things new.
Amen.

On The Wings Of A Prayer

[Jesus prayed,] "Protect them in your name that you have given me, so that they may be one, as we are one. While I was with them, I protected them in your name that you have given me."
John 17:11b-12a

Jenny is packing to go away. Our daughter is traveling to another continent on the other side of the globe for two years. There have been giant tugs of sadness in my heart. It feels very different from watching her pack for college where the telephone kept us connected weekly with tales of new adventures. This feels so very far away and out of range.

We have done all the necessary things, like checking in with family members, purchasing American essentials for the two-year stay and doing special things such as enjoying a movie and a special dessert. All that remains today is the final packing away of things left behind and getting on the airplane.

This time, more than any other that I can remember, has reminded me of the gift of prayer that is available to each of us. For there are times in life when there is no other way for us to care for one another. There is no other way for us to stay connected to each other.

A friend of ours wrote our daughter a note saying that she would add Jenny to her list of people that she prayed for each morning at her kitchen table during her morning devotions. She would pray for her until she was safely home again. The note touched me and brought an image to mind of people in the world literally connected to each other by prayer. Not in some simple name-raising for God's attention, but in some deep, spiritual way that love and good will could be transmitted through God to people everywhere.

It may be kin to the kind of prayer that Jesus prayed to God concerning his disciples as he was about to leave them. "Protect them in your name that you have given me, so that they may be one, as we are one. While I was with them, I protected them in your name that you have given me."

In a very secular world, where what you see is what you get, and where little is valued that cannot be held in the hand or put in the bank, hope in something as powerful as prayer is a rich blessing. That hope is not a naive hope that nothing bad could ever happen, because God certainly does not promise that. Rather it is the trust that love and concern are spiritual matters that come from God. They are transmitted by God and do not depend on physical presence, but on our spiritual nature to transcend time and place. Prayer keeps those spiritual matters healthy and alive.

That is our hope as we drive to the airport. It makes it possible for all of us to be filled with the joy of this new adventure as we return home to wait for the first letter.

Write soon, Jenny!

Loving God, we praise and thank you for the gift of prayer. Move us to be persistent in our praying so that we might be drawn closer to you and those we love. We pray in the name of your Son, Jesus. Amen.

The Gift Of "Being With"

[Jesus instructed his disciples saying, "Teach] them to obey everything that I have commanded you. And remember, I am with you always, to the end of the age." Matthew 28:20

The retreat setting was perfect. The pungent smell of smoke from the wood stove filled the large meeting room. Folks gathered in small circles for prayer. We had begun to trust each other enough to offer gifts. Two were offered: the first, a liturgical dance to the Prayer of St. Francis. The second, the singing of the Lord's Prayer, concluded this time of quiet prayer.

There was nothing very extraordinary about any of this. Nothing, except that the young man who had offered the gift of song was a young father who had spent most of the weekend supporting his wife who had just had a miscarriage. Many tears had been shared at the small round table as they shared their grief with friends. They had considered not staying at the retreat, but then claimed their need to be with friends at such a sad time.

Prayers for healing had been offered. I closed the time of prayer with traditional words of assurance. It was time for the Lord's Prayer. Rick stood solemnly behind his wife's chair and began to sing. But strong feelings prevailed, crowding that normally strong, clear tenor voice, which wavered and broke with emotion. It was then that we experienced the miracle. Such a small thing really, but I will never forget it.

Other worshippers began to sing along with the solo, their voices quiet and restrained. No one ventured to sing too loudly. They sang, they prayed, they listened. Mostly, they listened to Rick's voice leading in prayer. When Rick's voice grew faint, their voices rose. And as his voice grew stronger, more sure, they grew more silent. The congregation's voices offered their presence, always staying under the solo, literally holding the young man up with their love.

Very few were aware of the miracle; it went unnoticed by most, yet it has remained in my mind as a powerful example of the way we might always support each other in our lives and in our ministry. It is so tempting to take over, to give advice and to draw attention to ourselves rather than experiencing the miracle of the moment: simply "being with."

As we struggle to live with persons in conflict or crisis, we often miss the gifts they might bring to the community. "Being with" our sisters and our brothers is a fragile dance of knowing when to lead and when to follow. It is the dance of ministry, a dance of love.

I hope that Rick's family could feel our love and support. I also hope that the congregation could understand the significance of their gift of quiet singing.

Dear God, we experience your presence as we draw near to you. Stay close to us. May we stay close to one another. Amen.

SUMMER

Rituals Of The Heart

I will cause your name to be celebrated in all generations; therefore the peoples will praise you forever and ever. Psalm 45:17

When I was a pastor in southern California, I was asked to perform the marriage of Margaret, 79, and Howard, 82. These two dears had met after 50 years. Both had been long widowed and had been surprised again by love. As they set about the preparation of their wedding ceremony, Margaret, a piano teacher, wanted to be sure that we included her large collection of students — past and present — in the celebration.

Our little church was a busy part of the community and on this particular wedding Saturday, the local theater group was rehearsing *Oklahoma* in the church courtyard. They had been instructed to stop dancing and move into some of the classrooms for quieter rehearsing during the wedding and were used to such maneuvering.

Margaret arrived early with her maid-of-honor daughter, the car full of cake and flowers and all the fixings for a grand reception. Margaret was clearly in charge. Another carload of friends and relatives soon followed to help the bride and all was perfectly in place as the first guests began to arrive.

Although it was a small afternoon wedding, Margaret had requested that it be formal, so guests arrived in their proper wedding garments; ladies in their finest, men in tuxedos and small children scrubbed to a shine. I asked Margaret where Howard was. He was late but Margaret assured me that his son, who was the best-man, would be arriving with him any moment.

The wedding was scheduled for 1:00 p.m. At 1:30 p.m. the telephone rang. It was Howard. They had taken a wrong turn on the freeway. It would be at least two hours before they would arrive. With this news, the bride swung into action. "Good," she said, "then we'll just have the music first." So for the next hour or so, a parade of students made their way to the grand piano and played their current favorites. Tiny little five-year-olds, businessmen, teenagers — all took their place under the watchful eye of Margaret, their beloved teacher. When the music had been exhausted, Margaret said, "I know what we'll do. Let's have the reception now!"

So out of the sanctuary we trooped into the fellowship hall for cake, punch, mints and nuts. On her way through, Margaret met up with the *Oklahoma* cast and promptly invited them to join us. So, sweaty, scantily clad young dancers joined those in formal wedding garments. The reception went perfectly — the cutting of the cake, the toasting — all went without a hitch and all agreed that Howard would have been pleased — had he been there. Howard did arrive about 3:30 p.m. and we solemnly proceeded to the sanctuary for the simple ceremony. Old friends now, the *Oklahoma* cast stood at the back of the church, beaming at the radiant bride and groom.

Margaret taught me much that day. The most important rituals may not be those events which convention requires (such as the perfect wedding) but those that give rituals of the heart. Margaret was wise in knowing that God blesses those rituals that honor relationships and love.

Holy God, we praise and thank you for the rituals in our lives that keep our spirits healthy and our relationships strong. Bless our rituals performed in your name. Amen.

AUTUMN

Ritual Foods

He said to them, "I have eagerly desired to eat this Passover with you before I suffer; for I tell you, I will not eat it until it is fulfilled in the kingdom of God." Luke 22:15-16

Vacations are of two kinds — either you go somewhere you have never been and make lots of new memories or you retrace old memories in familiar places. I usually choose the latter. Reflecting on this year's vacation has set me thinking about the special foods — ritual foods— that are so much a part of our vacation plans.

I spoke with a friend who had traveled to California. She said she and a friend had gone out to eat every night. Each night was a rerun of a favorite place they used to go to when they both had lived in California. Though circumstances had changed for each of them, there was such comfort in sharing a hamburger at a favorite fast-food restaurant.

Last week, my friend and I retraced our old walking route, ending at a restaurant where we sat in "our" booth and recalled earlier years. The talking was easy as we looked at our lives then and now, reflecting on the changes. The orange juice and bran muffins fueled the conversation.

Our adult children also joined the trip back in time, as we made reservations at a favorite restaurant on the coast for brunch and talked of other visits there. We recalled the many family occasions celebrated in a Mexican restaurant as we enjoyed tacos and burritos. A trip back to our cabin in Wisconsin involved ritual foods as well:

cheese curds at our local cheese factory, root beer floats at the A&W root beer stand and brats from the small-town butcher.

It may be that our family just eats more than most, but it doesn't seem like all this eating is just about food. I think the ritual of eating and the memories it holds are so tightly bound together that the ritual food becomes a way to remember. Ritual food also becomes a way to express love and care. While staying in California with our adult son last week, we were greeted with a smorgasbord of family favorites: the right kind of cereal, cinnamon rolls with no raisins, cheese, sausage and fruit. None of the choices was remarkable except that they were chosen with us in mind. This adult child knew us well and wanted to tend to our needs. We felt welcomed and cared for. Ritual food is about paying attention to the needs of others. It is a way to show love for family and friends.

In our faith journey, we also enjoy ritual foods. Understanding that we are earthly human beings, we are given resources that connect our physical needs with our spiritual ones. These resources are always about memory and love. Some ritual food is obvious, such as the bread and the cup we share in communion or the fellowship meal we share during lovefeast.

Other foods aren't so obvious. A family meal that is shared can be a ritual meal, enabling loved ones to share memories and connect with the story of the larger family. A cup of coffee shared with a friend can be ritual food. A box of popcorn shared in a movie theater can be ritual food. Refreshment of the body and spirit comes in these ordinary events and I am grateful for vacations that especially offer such refreshment. The flood of memories and the nourishment of attention feed our hungry souls and feed us.

As we return to normal schedules, we will go back to eating right and eating light. Ritual foods are rich.

Nourishing God, we are so hungry and we come to you to be fed. Feed us, Jesus, and turn our hunger into a hunger for you and your word. Amen.

AUTUMN

Hands Tell A Story

How very good and pleasant it is when kindred live together in unity! It is like the precious oil on the head, running down upon the beard, on the beard of Aaron, running down over the collar of his robes. Psalm 133:1-2

"My body given for you."
Body in the bread, I hold in my hand
    and move from pew to pew to
    serve the outstretched hands.

The hands each tell the story
    of those who have gathered;
Porcelain hands of old ladies,
    holding cups of tea;
Slender hands of mid-life grace,
    poised and manicured;
Swarthy hands of strong men
    running huge equipment;
Chapped hands of young mothers
    callused hands of quilters,
Precise hands of accountants,
    skilled hands of nurses,
Hands of old loves,
    hands of new friends,
Arthritic hands,
    gardening hands,
Holding hands —

And I wonder if Christ were to grace
this supper, would he abandon
the water and the towel
and the washing of our feet?

And would he carry instead
a fragrant flask of oil
and take our hands in His
and gently rub the oil
into tired fingers and aching joints?
The oil of unity,
flowing down Aaron's beard;
The oil of anointing,
poured on the heads of kings;
The oil of comfort,
soothing the feet of Jesus.

It is our hands
that Christ must use each day
to heal the sick,
to comfort the sad,
to feed the hungry,
to play with babies,
to caress the painful body.

It is these hands that need
to be nourished and soothed.
For these hungry, reaching hands
The Body is the bread.
"My body given for you."

Incarnate God, help us to know what it means to be the body of Christ. Make our hands become your hands, to heal, to soothe, and to love. Amen.

AUTUMN

COMMUTING WITH A TRAVEL PAL

I do not understand my own actions. For I do not do what I want, but I do the very thing I hate.
Romans 7:15

For the past seven years, I have been making a two-hour commute twice a week. It is a wonderful journey, through rolling farmlands with pristine white outbuildings on prosperous farms. I loved watching the seasons change as horse-drawn farm implements plowed, then planted, and finally picked the fields of corn. The time passed quickly as my eyes feasted on the view. At least the morning trips passed quickly. But sometimes the time dragged on the Wednesday and Friday afternoon return trips. The setting sun would blaze through the front windshield, making it impossible to see. I would be tired and would begin ticking off the exits.

The worst part of the trip home was the last 25 minutes. It was one small town after another on a curvy country road, made treacherous by buggies and slow-moving farm machinery. That's when I would look for my traveling buddy. The anticipation of our brief encounter would leave me smiling the rest of the way home.

It took me several months to establish the routine and to remember which town he was in, then which street, and finally, which house. But I soon knew the spot. There he would be, out on his front porch, a middle-aged man, wearing a baseball cap and work clothes. He invariably sat on a chair with his feet up on the railing of the porch. Sometimes he was talking on the phone, but most times he was just sitting on the porch watching the cars go by. It didn't matter when I drove by; from as early as 5:00 o'clock to as late as 7:00, he always seemed to be there.

I began to look forward to seeing him. After about a year, I started to wave at him as I drove by. I was sure that by this time, he was beginning to recognize my small car. I could imagine him going back into the house and asking, "Who do we know that has an aqua car?"

Except in the coldest of winter weather, he was out there on the porch and after a couple of years of seeing me pass twice a week, he began to wave, tentatively at first, just a slight movement of the wrist. This slight response prompted me to wave more vigorously, which over the months got a more energetic response from my buddy. For the last couple of years now, I have begun greeting my friend with a friendly honk of my horn.

While all of this has been transpiring, I have reflected on this strange ritual and why it has so delighted me. Perhaps it was the mystery of who this person was. Perhaps it was my need for some personal relationship in a strange town. Perhaps it was just some kind of cosmic gesture that affirmed that we were both human beings on the planet. Whatever it was, it clearly enriched my travel home each evening. I have no clue whether my travel buddy pondered anything at all or if he even saw any kind of pattern or ritual in the waving of this odd woman.

Recently, I moved, so that my commute is no longer necessary. As I participated in the farewells that accompany such a move, it did occur to me that I should perhaps stop and say good-bye to my buddy. For several weeks, I considered it. In fact, I even planned what I would say. So on the last day, with my heart in my hand, I slowed the car to be ready to find a safe place to stop and run up to speak with him.

But on this day, on a rainy, cold Friday afternoon, he wasn't there. I didn't say good-bye. I wish I had.

Merciful God, forgive us for the times that we thwart our good intentions. The good that we know to do often does not get done. We are sorry. Amen.

AUTUMN

A Dark And Stormy Day

For the Son of Man came to seek out and to save the lost. Luke 19:10

It was a dark and stormy day. I headed west on the Pennsylvania Turnpike on my way to Kentucky for a conference. My tiny, very old car pressed on valiantly, withstanding the gusts of wind. The windshield wipers did their best to keep the window clear of the sheets of rain. It was not a pleasant morning to be traveling.

About an hour west of Harrisburg, my radio stopped. I thought that was strange, but attributing it to the weather, I put a tape in. It didn't work either. A minute later, the wipers began to slow down. Since I am a dedicated *Car Talk* fan, it didn't take me too long to figure out that I was losing power, quickly. A sign read *Service Plaza* two miles. So I turned off the lights and stuck my head out the window to limp the two long miles to the off ramp. I made it to the gas pumps where the car proudly died, having delivered me safely. One phone call to AAA and a tow truck was on its way. I waited in the service station with a cup of coffee.

In a short amount of time, the tow truck arrived. Out stepped Kevin, a young, no-nonsense kind of guy who greeted me and laid out the plan. I should stay inside and he would hook the car up and call ahead for parts. I felt guilty and rather useless as he carefully rigged up the apparatus to tow my car. The rain had let up a bit, but he still was getting soaked as he worked. I noticed the precision in the way he did things, reaching purposely from one to another, using this tool and then that piece of equipment. Each compartment lid was carefully latched and I was reminded of flight attendants securing the overhead compartments, preparing for takeoff.

Soon I was in the front seat of his warm truck on my way to the next town, with my little aqua car being dragged along behind me. It was a 30-minute drive, he said, so we began to get acquainted. He told me that he was 22 years old and had always wanted to work with cars and with people. He had never traveled farther than the Pennsylvania Turnpike, east or west, which suited him just fine, he said.

He then began a delightful tale about an earlier call. He had been summoned to a group of hunters who had locked their keys in the car. They had a cellular phone so they called for help. He described the terrain where they had been hunting and how he had followed instructions from their phone to travel deeper and deeper into the mountains to find them. The roads kept getting smaller and smaller until finally he found the stranded hunters.

We chatted for some time, about our common back surgeries and exercise programs. Then he turned to me and said, "You know, I love my job." He quickly added a disclaimer, "Oh, there are some folks who get mad at me because their car broke down, so those aren't very pleasant. But most days, I love my job." I asked him what he loved about it. He replied, "People are so glad to see me arrive. They are in trouble and I can do something to help them. All I do every day is save people."

That's not a bad way to make a living. Kevin wouldn't have cared about the psychobabble of the dangers and codependent behavior of persons who need to rescue people. Nor would he have been very impressed with the theological concerns of saving people. He just saw in the saving a job, a purpose and a good, honest way to be a human being.

Saving God, you save us when we are lost and alone. Through your Son Jesus, we are given second chances, rebirth and the ability to start over. Thank you, O God of our salvation. Amen.

STAYING OPEN

But I will stay in Ephesus until Pentecost, for a wide door for effective work has opened to me, and there are many adversaries. 1 Corinthians 16:8-9

I arrived at the airport very early to make sure that I could get a good seat. My flight time came and went. We were told that there would be a delay because of engine trouble, so we settled back to wait while mechanics hurried back and forth between the terminal and our airplane. Two hours passed and we were all getting hungry and irritable. Finally, we heard the announcement that the tiny little restaurant in the airport would be opened so that we could get something to eat. The tiny dining room had ten tables overlooking the gate where our wounded airplane received treatment. I was escorted to a table for two and began reading the menu. Very soon a waitress approached my table and asked if I would mind if someone joined me since the seating was so limited. I certainly didn't mind.

My luncheon companion was charming and the time passed quickly. By the time we had eaten and waited a short time to board, we were fast friends and chose to continue our conversation on our one-hour flight. By this time, we had exchanged all the important family data about children, husbands and places we had lived and were getting down to more interesting matters. She began by telling me that she always tried to sit with someone if she was traveling alone. She said she met the most interesting people that way. Then she took it one step further. She said that she tried to be open to these encounters because she found that God often sent folks her way to raise a particular challenge for her or to provide some new opportunity to learn and grow. Sometimes God sent wonderful surprises. She said she had recently experienced an event like that, if I would like to hear the story.

The story had happened a few weeks before as she was turning 50. She had decided that she wanted to do something to celebrate this important milestone in her life. She and her husband were avid hikers but she had always yearned to go rock climbing. Her husband wasn't interested and after several unsuccessful attempts, she had given up on the idea, thinking that maybe she was just too old anyway.

On her birthday, a beautiful warm fall day, she and her husband had risen early to see if they could get in a game of golf before the course got busy. Even though it was early, nothing was available unless they wanted to join a couple who were just about ready to tee off. Her husband reluctantly agreed and off they went. The two couples found that they enjoyed each other for the nine holes and went back to the clubhouse for some breakfast and more conversation. They exchanged telephone numbers for another golf date and as they turned to go, the man said, "By the way, if you know of anyone who might be interested in learning to rock climb, let us know. We have a weekend training school and there still should be a number of good weekends left before cold weather."

Now, most folks would call this luck or coincidence, but my friend saw God in this. She really trusted that if she did her part, which was to remain open, curious and eager for new adventures, God would do the rest. She described the ministries and mission projects that God had called her to and the curious way so many of them came about. Old friends now, we parted reluctantly at the gate. Somewhere soon, I bet she'll be rock climbing.

God of surprises, help us to keep open so that we can be ready for your challenges and opportunities to grow. When we are set in our ways, nudge us to be willing to try a new thing. Amen.

AUTUMN

Serving God And Nissan

[Jesus said:] "No one can serve two masters; for a slave will either hate the one and love the other, or be devoted to the one and despise the other. You cannot serve God and wealth. Matthew 6:24

Somewhere in southern California, there is a pale blue '84 Datsun. Its odometer reads 187,653 miles. The seats are bare pieces of metal with small tufts of plaid vinyl upholstery that stick to one's clothing when exiting the front seat. There had been one hubcap but it is now also gone, along with the air conditioning, the fuel gauge, the radio and the windshield wipers. The trunk has a ragged hole in it, looking like someone tried to open it with a very large can opener. Gray duct tape feebly attempts to cover the hole, while struggling to keep the infrequent California rain from filling the trunk.

When our son turned 16 and got his driver's license, he inherited this family relic from his older sister. It got him to school and to work quite regularly, often with equal portions of gas and oil. This fall, while in college and alive with the heady notion of his first full-time job, our son's impatience with the old reliable increased. He began to dream of buying a new truck. The weekly telephone calls from California sounded something like this:

Week 1 – Dad, I looked at this beautiful new Nissan truck. The dealer said that he would give me $500 for the Datsun. I think I can make enough to meet the payments. What do you think?

Week 2 – Mom, I bought the truck. It's shiny black and gray and I can't believe it's really mine. I'm so happy but it's scary to look ahead and think about all the payments!

Week 3 – My truck is absolutely perfect except that it doesn't have a stereo in it, but I can get this great deal on a used one from my friend. He says he'll take $80 for it, but he needs the money right away.

Week 4 – Do you guys know anything about security systems? I'm thinking of buying one because I'm afraid someone will rip off my new cool stereo.

Week 5 – What a week! Got three parking tickets because I haven't wanted to park in the apartment complex parking lot. The woman next to me parks too close and I'm afraid she will ding my truck.

The Gospel of Matthew reminds us that "No one can serve two masters.... You cannot serve God and wealth" (Matthew 6:24 NRSV). When that wealth gets changed into a beautiful new Nissan truck, the message becomes clear. Those things we possess seem to take on a life of their own and they begin to possess us. Material possessions are usually quite innocent but they are demanding. They demand our attention and our care. They become a priority. Sometimes they keep us from following a goal or from caring for others. Sometimes they keep us from serving God. We cannot serve God and Nissan trucks.

God, we confess that our attentions get diverted away from following your will. Our material things control us and try to fill the empty spots in our lives. Fill us, Lord. Amen.

AUTUMN

Just One Hour

Be careful then how you live, not as unwise people but as wise, making the most of the time, because the days are evil. Ephesians 5:15-16

This is the time of year we gain an hour by setting our clocks back. That is an amazing gift. Think about it. Being given an hour, 60 minutes — free — with no strings attached. The potential of such a gift is enormous, if we could use our imaginations.

Most of us slept the hour away since we changed our clocks before we went to bed and we needed the sleep. But what if we decided to set the clock back on Tuesday in the afternoon, say three o'clock? We could declare a time out, an hour that wasn't in our appointment book. It didn't appear on any calendar so it couldn't be filled with meetings or other duties. It would be a free gift to every person and each could decide how to use the hour.

What if we would leave work for an hour and go home and play with our kids?

What if we would use the hour to have tea with someone who is feeling lonely?

What if we would use the hour to clean out a closet and find good clothing to take to a shelter or thrift shop?

What if we went to a grocery store and bought a bag of nonperishable items to take to a food pantry?

What if everyone in the neighborhood got together for a cup of coffee and got to know one another?

What if city workers could meet informally with their constituents, with no agenda, just to listen?

What if government officials could spend an hour listening to their conscience concerning an issue or cause?

What if two or three world leaders could use the hour to dream about peace?

One hour is not much time, but it could become a wonderful resource for the well-being of the community. It could make a difference but in reality, it is impossible to give such a gift. Or is it?

I challenge each of us to reclaim that hour we wasted sleeping and use it for good. You'll know what you can do. But do it soon — time flies by so quickly that April will be here before we know it and we'll have to give that hour back.

Timeless God, we govern our lives by the clock and calendar. It is how we live. Help us to measure time as you measure time and help us to be patient. Amen.

AUTUMN

Reasons To Be Thankful

Rejoice always, pray without ceasing, give thanks in all circumstances; for this is the will of God in Christ Jesus for you. 1 Thessalonians 5:16-18

It is that time of year again — time to give thanks. Such a small thing really, but I get uncomfortable when it is time to make lists of things for which I am thankful. It is tempting to sit in my comfortable home in my free country and name all of my favorite things. Smugness and arrogance are just around the corner of any such list.

The biblical text reminds us to "give thanks in all circumstances; for this is the will of God in Christ Jesus for you." Giving thanks in all circumstances is a hard thing to do. When terrible things happen to me, it is not easy to be thankful to God. But I have discovered that after a time, when the terrible things have passed, it is a little easier to be thankful for even those terrible things.

This year, I am making a different kind of list. I think it is time to be thankful for the things for which I haven't asked, things that I haven't wanted, things that I thought would ruin my life.

It has taken decades of living to know enough to be thankful for these things.

1. I am thankful that as a young girl I lived on a farm because when I am driving on a beautiful country road with the strong smell of manure in the air, I know how valuable that process is for growing crops and I don't mind the smell quite so much.

2. I am thankful that I played third clarinet in my high school band. It taught me to feel proud of doing something tedious and uninspir-

ing because it contributed to the whole. It taught me how to be part of a team.

3. I am thankful that in my senior year in high school, during a drama program in front of the whole student body, I lost my place in the middle of a scene of a play and stood dumbly, looking out at all those blank faces, trying desperately to remember my lines. It taught me never to underestimate the courage and skill it takes to get up in front of a crowd of people.

4. I am thankful that for some inexplicable medical reason we weren't able to have children biologically but were given the gifts and challenges of adopting four wonderful children.

5. I am thankful for the coldest, most bitter winter and the hottest most miserable summer because then a mild spring day and a crisp fall evening become inexpressible treasures.

6. I am thankful for the most difficult people in my life because they have pushed and changed me in ways that I find to be helpful. Although I often wish that they would all go away, I find that I have learned a great deal from each of them.

7. I am thankful for human events and movements that sweep me up and challenge my old world views even though they can be prickly and unnerving.

8. I am thankful I have not received some of the things that I have most prayed for because I have learned about God's timing versus my urgency and the difference between them.

9. I am thankful for Thanksgivings in the past when turkeys were dry as sawdust and the cat stepped in the pumpkin pie because it takes a lot of pressure off me to prepare the perfect Thanksgiving feast this year.

Happy Thanksgiving!

Thank you, God, for our lives and for the gifts and graces that make us your unique creatures. Forgive us for times when we have forgotten to be thankful. Amen.

AUTUMN

Threads That Bind Us All

By the tender mercy of our God, the dawn from on high will break upon us, to give light to those who sit in darkness and in the shadow of death, to guide our feet into the way of peace. Luke 1:78-79

The airport was a flurry of winter coats, brightly colored lights and people in a hurry. At the waiting area between Gate 7 and Gate 8, in the midst of all the holiday travelers, a young couple huddled together. The young woman's face revealed a turned-down mouth and quivery chin. She held a tissue to her nose. A festive Christmas sweater did nothing to cheer up the sad face. She had pulled the sleeves down over her hands as if she were cold. The young man kept patting her back and shoulders. He tenderly tucked a lock of hair behind her ear, talking quietly to her. The announcement for his plane to Baltimore caused them both to rise in unison.

With the crowd they were nudged along to the gate, still holding each other tightly. They kissed. People walked on either side of them barely taking notice. She clung to his neck until he finally broke away and walked through the gate just as it was being closed by the attendant. She didn't turn from the gate but walked the few feet to the window and watched him walk out to the small jet. She watched as they put his bag underneath the plane. She watched as they closed the door. She watched as the tiny plane turned around. She watched as it taxied down the runway, picked up speed and finally lifted into the air. She watched until the tiny plane was just a small speck in the gray afternoon. She watched until she couldn't see it any longer and still she stood there, as if standing there would keep them connected.

Some fragile thread was reaching out through the wintry sky, trailing along behind the plane so that she wasn't being left alone. Turning from the window would break the thread that bound them together.

Later, the attendant saw her, still standing at the window, with her sleeves pulled down over her hands. As he began to prepare for the next flight, he glanced her way. He wondered how old she was. Probably about the age of his own daughter, he guessed. Whether it was the season, or whether it was because she reminded him of Emily, whatever the reason, he walked over to the snack bar and bought two steaming cups of hot chocolate. He approached her quietly, not wanting to frighten her.

"Miss, are you all right? How about sharing a cup of hot chocolate with me? I am about to take my break."

She turned finally, slowly, her eyes red from crying. Her sleeves hung long and droopy and little wads of tissue filled each fist. "Oh, I didn't realize that anyone was here. I just needed a little time." She smiled dimly and reached toward the warm cup of comfort. "Thanks. It will keep me warm when I go out to get the car."

They sat on the plastic sling chairs, sipping their hot drinks and talking about the things that strangers in airports talk about: where her young man was going, how late the attendant had to work, and how much Christmas shopping they had left to do.

But if you looked very closely, you might be able to see the fragile thread that floated between them. It was gold and it sparkled in the lights of the Christmas decorations. It was not the same thread that connected the young couple but it was there nevertheless. It circled above the two drinking cocoa, it swooped over to the snack bar where the waitress smiled and hummed *Jingle Bells*. Later, it followed the young woman as she started down the escalator. She pulled the scarf up around her neck to keep out the wind, and put her hands in her pockets. The gold Christmas ribbon trailed behind her red parking lights as she started for home.

Tender God, we thank you for moments when we become better human beings than we really are. Inspire us to allow ourselves to have soft hearts and tender souls. In the name of your Son. Amen.

AUTUMN

A Good Time To Look Up

When I look at your heavens, the work of your fingers, the moon and the stars that you have established; what are human beings that you are mindful of them, mortals that you care for them?
Psalm 8:3-4

It was the first Sunday in Advent, the beginning of the church year, and the preacher had begun the familiar preparation sermon. "Prepare the way of the Lord," the preacher toned from the high pulpit. "All who have ears let them hear." Directly over the preacher's head was a traditional Moravian star, nearly six feet across, lit for the first time just minutes before. As the preacher moved into his second page, the huge star suddenly jolted and slipped several inches from the ceiling where it was attached. Though it didn't fall farther, it twirled ominously over the head of the preacher. He stopped midsentence and looked out at the congregation. "It is apparent to me that not one of you in this entire church is looking in my direction." Following the gazes of the parishioners, he looked up and quickly stepped back out of the line of the potentially descending star. Ushers flew into action and after several minutes it was determined that the star was secure and the service could continue.

Certainly the descent of the Advent star became the sermon that day and perhaps more importantly, the star caused the congregation to look up. It is what that first star over Bethlehem did too. "They looked up and saw a star, shining in the east beyond them far; And to the earth it gave great light, and so it continued both day and night. Noel, noel, Born is the King of Israel."

Looking up is good work for the first Sunday in Advent. Looking up is also good work for the coming of a new calendar year. When I was in junior high and feeling particularly adventuresome, I used to join my friends to take the bus uptown to the capitol square in Madison, Wisconsin. We delighted in standing on the sidewalk and pretending to look intently at something high up on the capitol building. Though we were just a bunch of kids, it was very hard for most folks to pass by without looking up too. When that happened we would giggle and move on.

Perhaps there is in the human spirit an inner capacity for looking up, for looking beyond ourselves. There are many good reasons for looking up. Psalm 8 offers a wonderful "looking up" reason. "When I look at your heavens, the work of your fingers, the moon and the stars that you have established; what are human beings that you are mindful of them, mortals that you care for them?" Psalm 8:3-4

Looking up reminds us of how small we are compared to the universe, to all of creation. It helps us to be humble. Looking up gives us the feeling that we are part of something so big and cosmic that we can do anything. It gives us power and confidence. Looking up lifts us out of ourselves for a little while so that we can try some new thing, or take a risk, or rise beyond what is usually expected. It energizes us. Looking up may be a way of connecting with those we have loved who have died. It gives us hope.

Looking up is transforming because that is where we might imagine God to be, and looking up connects us with God in some new way. It strengthens our faith. Looking up is not idealistic or impractical because we look up with our two feet firmly planted on the ground where we need to be. It is a good way to start a new year.

So climb a hill. Take a walk downtown. Look out your window. Keep looking up.

Transcendent God, we know that you are not a God up in the sky, but we still look up in worship and praise. We are grateful that you came to earth for us. Amen.

THE TERRIBLE "TOOS"

Likewise the Spirit helps us in our weakness; for we do not know how to pray as we ought, but that very Spirit intercedes with sighs too deep for words. And God, who searches the heart, knows what is the mind of the Spirit, because the Spirit intercedes for the saints according to the will of God. Romans 8:26-27

Just a few shopping days till Christmas. So how are things going for you? It is the blessed Christmas holiday and it may be the least likely time for anyone to actually experience God. The terrible *toos* often get in the way — we are *too* tired, *too* busy, *too* poor, or *too* rich.

The paradox of the nativity, the unlikeliness of the incarnation, the irrational experience of a baby God in a manger, requires something new from us. At this time, as much as that other unlikely holy time, Easter, we need to scratch the surface of our lives and leave some holes for God to enter in. We sing about finding room for God. We pray that we might welcome the Christ-child this year.

There is still time to make this Christmas different from other holidays. Here are some improbable ways to approach the last remaining days of Advent:

Doing nothing is doing something. This is revolutionary and we don't even accept this notion in our faith lives, but the idea has merit. Doing nothing, even in very short increments of time, can be life changing.

Do one thing at a time. Actually being attentive to the task at hand may even be more efficient, but that wouldn't be the reason to try it.

Paying attention to one thing at a time may clear our minds and hearts to hear and experience some new thing.

Let your troubles get their own lives. This is not suggesting that you become irresponsible, nor is it about letting your worries become your life, but learning to live with them, perhaps to live around them. Romans 8:28 is often translated, "all things work together for good." A variation can be read, "all things intermingle with good." The bad stuff takes its place alongside the good stuff. The people who walked in darkness have seen a great light. And here is the hope. The light wins.

Urge underachievement. Try lowering your goals for Christmas by just one batch of cookies. It might change your life.

Aim for imperfection. Being perfect is always overrated. This year, aim for slightly less than perfect. Aim for a good enough Christmas and you'll probably have one.

Do one new thing that doesn't cost anything but makes your soul giggle. Watch an old Christmas classic or read one. Make paper chains. Go for a ride and see the lights.

Any one of these suggestions might be helpful because we are preparing for a miracle, for a mystery. Like butterflies and rainbows, miracles usually don't happen when we try harder, go faster, buy more or get bigger. Advent is about not trying so hard, about going slower, about getting smaller — smaller like a tiny baby. Advent is about making holes in our souls, so that God can enter. Advent is about clearing out the debris and making room in our hearts.

Romans 8:26-27 offers the help we need for Advent: "The Spirit intercedes for the saints… God searches the heart…." God's Spirit moves in us with murmurings that have no words and God is always searching for us, looking in the broken places, in the places where we have scratched our surface. In the imperfection of our Advent preparation, the perfect will appear, the perfect God-baby born again in us.

Blessed Infant, in the midst of all the glitter of this holiday, help us to see your pure love and holiness. May the melody of your love sing in our hearts and shine in our faces. Amen.

AUTUMN

A "Good Enough" Christmas

On entering the house, they saw the child with Mary his mother; and they knelt down and paid him homage. Then, opening their treasure chests, they offered him gifts of gold, frankincense, and myrrh. Matthew 2:11

For almost 30 years I have trudged to the grocery story sometime late in November to purchase my personal copies of the Christmas issues of *Family Circle* and *Women's Day.* I have picked up a couple of other magazines, too, and each year I am promised "fast fabulous touches for a beautiful holiday," "Christmas made easy," "Tips to make Christmas happier, saner and more meaningful," and "130 holiday ideas for making the whole season a very special time." You don't have to be a magazine consumer to be tempted by these promises. You've seen it on TV and in the newspapers. You've seen and heard the commercials.

We all want to do everything that we can do to make this the best Christmas ever. But in spite of all the magazines, in spite of all our efforts, the brutal truth is: Toys of destruction will be best sellers for the birthday of the Prince of Peace. There will still be poor, hungry people on Christmas Day afternoon. Nations will still be at war and still threatening the lives of their people. Families will still be in pain and estranged from each other. Communities will still mourn for the murdered bodies of their young men and women caught in the plight of the city. There will still be those who will try to kill themselves or someone else on the happiest night of the year. And in the light of Christmas morning, amidst all the clutter of too many presents and not enough joy, we will blame it on God. Why didn't God do the magic? Why didn't God make it happen on the birth of the Christ child?

Christmas can be a difficult time, for it is a time that we expose ourselves. We keep trying to have an A+ Christmas in a B- world. And we keep getting disappointed. We keep trying to celebrate Christmas by just telling half of the story, the sweet part. But Christmas is not a holiday for the meek and mild. It is for the courageous and strong. It takes courage to see through the beauty of a candle's flame or the light of a star to the cross that is also part of Christmas.

In psychological jargon there is a term for a healthy environment that produces normal healthy adults. The psychologists call it a "good enough" environment. It isn't perfect but it is good enough to produce the desired effect. That's what I would wish for us this Advent — a Good Enough Christmas.

May it be good enough to give us a tiny taste of peace that will sustain us in troubled times ahead. May it be good enough to offer a ray of hope for the coming year. May it be good enough to fill up some empty place in our hearts, some small place that may be broken and in need of healing. May it be good enough to slip into our hectic lives that we can draw it back into our lives when joy has left us. And may we be able to resist some of the commercial hype of the season that guarantees that we will be disappointed, that Christmas won't quite be all that we need it to be. May we find the real life and death event of the Christ child — a birthday good enough to be the hope of the world.

Holy Christ-child, your birth causes us to look at our own lives. Your death and resurrection give our lives meaning. Help us to keep you in our celebration of Christmas. Amen.

AUTUMN

God Offers A Spiritual New Year

And the one who was seated on the throne said, "See, I am making all things new." Also he said, "Write this, for these words are trustworthy and true." Revelation 21:5

When it comes to choosing Christmas gifts, calendars are perhaps a boring choice, but calendars are the perfect generic gift. There are no sizes required, you don't have to worry if people already have one and calendars are usually very easy to wrap. If you do know a particular interest of the recipient, you can usually find the right match. Calendars are the perfect choice for Christmas. In addition, though folks may prefer one set of pictures over another, we can assume that every single person on our list will need a new calendar six days after Christmas.

The calendar business is a flourishing business. Each year there seem to be more on the market. Some are works of art with each month containing a picture ready for framing. Some offer the recipient instructions for craft projects or recipes for mouth-watering dishes that are presented in pictures of feast-laden tables.

Perhaps most of us give and receive calendars without any deep thought or intent. But I'm going to suggest that giving calendars can become a symbol of what we would really like to give our friends and family, a brand new year, a year with unlimited possibility, of new beginnings and a way for the past year to be past and forgotten.

Starting a new year is part of the human experience. But starting a new year in January often seems strange. Some of us who spend most of our lives in academic settings feel the natural rhythm of the fall semester and feel like the year should start in September. Some of us who are moved by the first sweet flowers of spring think that the year should start then with the rhythm of the seasons being the time-keeper. But in this culture, we start over in January. After a food-filled week of too much activity, in that sleepy aftermath of Christmas, comes the new year. Whether we are ready or not, the new year comes and calls for celebration.

And as part of that celebration, we put up our new calendars. We cannot be so naive to think that the hanging up of a new calendar will fix our lives. But perhaps like so many things that we do in our religious lives, a new calendar becomes a metaphor, a symbol for us. It stands for that which God has already done, what God continually does. God continually offers us a new start.

"Behold, I make all things new" is a promise from Revelation. Behold, God makes even our most spoiled past months a part of our past. God offers us the opportunity to leave the past back in the old year. It is a year that has brought its own joy and its own sadness. But behold, we are given a brand new year, as new as a newborn baby, all innocent and unspoiled.

Our calendar comes that way, all fresh and clean and unmarked. As you put up your new calendar, claim your new life. And rather than filling up the days and months with lists and resolutions, perhaps we might receive the year that is given us, as it comes to us, as empty pages full of potential and hope.

Happy New Year!

God of the ages, we praise you for new beginnings, new years and new selves. Look with favor as we offer ourselves to you in this new year. In Christ's name we pray. Amen.

About The Author

Kay Ward was born and raised in Madison, Wis., and learned from her Irish father how to appreciate the telling of a good story very early in her life. As a young girl, she began attending Sunday School at Lakeview Moravian Church in Madison. It was there, under the joyful ministry of Bishop Milo Loppnow that she learned of God and found a spiritual home.

Her teen years brought the beginnings of a call to "full-time service to serve her Lord and Savior Jesus Christ" (a phrase often repeated at commitment services at youth camps and conferences.) That call was confusing because it would be years before the Moravian Church would ordain women. A way to answer that call seemed to be teaching, so Kay attended Carroll College in Waukesha, Wis., receiving a B.A. in education and religion.

She and her high school sweetheart, Aden, were married during her senior year at Carroll. Kay taught 6th grade in Madison for a number of years. In the late 60s, Aden entered the ordained ministry and Kay became a stay-home mom.

When the time was right, Kay entered Moravian Theological Seminary and earned a M.Div. degree, receiving ordination in 1979. Serving in team ministry, the Wards served Moravian churches in Indiana and California. While in California, Kay earned a D.Min. from the School of Theology at Claremont.

A lifelong dream of combining theology and education was realized in 1990 as Kay took a position at Moravian Seminary in Bethlehem, Pa., where she has taught Christian Education, directed the continuing education program and where she currently serves as director of seminary advancement.

In 1998 at the Moravian Church – Northern Province Synod, Kay was elected as the first woman bishop of the Moravian Church and was consecrated at a service in November of that year. Bishop Milo Loppnow was the presiding bishop at the service.

Kay and her husband have four grown children and, as this book is being written, are awaiting the birth of their first grandchild.

"If you think I had a lot of stories to write about my family, wait till I am a grandmother," Kay commented with her ever-present smile.

In addition to providing great ideas for stories, Kay's family and friends sustain her with their love.

"I am rich in family — husband, sons, daughters, son-in-law, mother, sister, nephews, in-laws, cousins, aunt and uncles — who provide help when it's time to work, play when it's time to play, and love all the time.

"I am rich in friends — in Madison, Nazareth, Door County, Wisconsin Rapids, Winston-Salem, Mequon, Waukesha, Boston, Bethlehem and Lititz and in many other places — who listen patiently as I tell my stories over and over and who still want to be my friend."

Kay continues to write for the *Express Times* newspaper in Easton, Pa., where the stories in this book were originally published in a column format. These stories have found new life as meditations under the guidance of Roxann Miller, director of Communication, Moravian Church in America. Kay is currently working on a collection of short stories.

Index To Scriptures